MAKE YOUR WILL
THE RIGHT WAY

In the same series

First Time Buyer: First Time Seller
First Time Tenant
Divorce
When Someone Dies

Uniform with this book

Where to find *Right Way*

Elliot *Right Way* take pride in our editorial quality, accuracy and value-for-money. Booksellers everywhere can rapidly obtain any *Right Way* book for you. If you have been particularly pleased with any one title, do please mention this to your bookseller as personal recommendation helps us enormously.

Please send to the address on the back of the title page opposite, a stamped, self-addressed envelope if you would like a copy of our *free catalogue*. Alternatively, you may wish to browse through our extensive range of informative titles arranged by subject on the Internet at **www.right-way.co.uk**

We welcome views and suggestions from readers as well as from prospective authors; do please write to us or e-mail:
info@right-way.co.uk

MAKE YOUR WILL THE RIGHT WAY

Joyce Bennell

RIGHT WAY

Typeset in 11 pt Times by Letterpart Ltd., Reigate, Surrey.
Printed and bound in Great Britain by Cox & Wyman Ltd., Reading, Berkshire.

The *Right Way* series is published by Elliot Right Way Books, Brighton Road, Lower Kingswood, Tadworth, Surrey, KT20 6TD, U.K. For information about our company and the other books we publish, visit our website at www.right-way.co.uk

CONTENTS

INTRODUCTION

This book will help you to make your will. It explains all the requirements for a legally valid will in England and Wales and points out the problems that can arise if a will isn't made properly.

The book covers the law in England and Wales only. The law in other parts of the British Isles is different in many respects and is not covered. Anyone (including a foreign national) who is aged 18 or older and who lives in England and Wales, or who owns property here, can make a will under English law. Conversely, residents of England and Wales may make wills in other parts of the world if they own property there.

The law relating to wills and the administration of the affairs of deceased people is vast and complicated. The leading work on the subject of wills extends to two large volumes and many thousands of words. In a book this size it is impossible to go into the same depth or to cover each and every situation which may arise. However, if your affairs are straightforward, you should be able to make a valid will following the guidance within these pages. If your affairs are more complicated, you will still find the information helpful. It will help you to gather your thoughts and map out your wishes before seeking professional advice on the actual drafting of your will.

The book also covers the basic process of administration of a deceased's estate. 'Estate' is the term used to describe the assets the deceased leaves and the liabilities to be settled. The term 'administration' means the collecting in of the assets, settlement of the liabilities, winding up of the tax affairs of the deceased and paying out the money due to the beneficiaries.

Throughout the book the masculine includes the feminine and vice versa unless otherwise stated.

1

WHAT IS A WILL?

We have probably all heard of wills and perhaps been involved with the estate of a deceased relative but how many of us know exactly what the term 'will' means? In fact, a will is the most important document you will ever sign in your lifetime and is the one document about whose contents you cannot be consulted when it really matters, i.e. after your death. The definition used when I was at law school was, 'A will is a declaration with due formality of the dispositions a testator intends to take effect on his death and which is revocable until then.' The Trustee Act 2000 defines a will as, 'a document by which a person (called "the testator") appoints executors to administer his estate after his death and directs the manner in which it is to be distributed to the beneficiaries he specifies.' In legal parlance the term for a female who writes a will is 'testatrix'. In the coming chapters you will see how a will should be constructed, the formalities for its signing and storage and a little about what happens after your death.

Do I need a will?
The answer to this is an unequivocal 'Yes'. Everyone should make a will but the message does not seem to be getting through to the public at large. It is a fact that the majority of people in England and Wales still die without making a will. The reasons for this would appear to be a mixture of misconceptions as to what happens to a person's money, etc., on death, coupled with a superstitious

fear of tempting fate. In other words, there is a widely held superstitious belief that making a will means you will bring about your own demise. In fact, it is better to make a will while you are fit and healthy and, more importantly, while your mental capacity is beyond question.

Let us first examine some of the common beliefs surrounding wills and why these are incorrect.

I am married so my husband/wife will get everything
This apparently widely held belief is not correct. If you die without making a will, the law declares you to be 'intestate' and decides where your money goes. In some instances, this can be to the Crown. The Appendix shows the division of the estate according to the intestacy laws. You will see that your spouse will not necessarily receive all of your estate and may well have to share it with your children and/or other relatives. This will often be contrary to your wishes and may also cause untold distress to the bereaved spouse.

The law of intestacy does not recognise the claims of stepchildren or cohabitees either. If your stepchildren have lived with you since they were very small, you may well regard them as your children and wish to see them have something from your estate. Without the existence of a will giving them specific provision, they will be left out. Likewise, a co-habitee is entitled to nothing under the intestacy laws.

Making a will also gives you the opportunity to include a legacy (a sum of money or a specific object) to a friend or to a favourite charitable cause. It also provides an opportunity to control the age at which your children receive your money or to make special arrangements for a child with disabilities. If you have children under 18, you can appoint testamentary guardians to take care of them if you should die.

If you make a will before you get married, it will be revoked, by operation of law, on your wedding day. This happens even if the person who benefits under your will is the person you later marry. If you wish to make a will immediately prior to your marriage, then it needs to include special wording to avoid automatic revocation.

I am not worth anything
It is quite common for people to be worth more dead than alive. Add up the totals of your life assurance policies, your death in service benefits and so on. What about your car, your house and the antique furniture your grand-mother bequeathed you? The total may well surprise you. Anyway it is your money, regardless of how small the sum, and you should be the one to say where it goes on your death.

It costs a lot of money to make a will
Will-drafting is not for the faint-hearted. It requires care-ful thought and clear expression. The law relating to wills and succession is very complicated and the pitfalls for the unwary are numerous. It is often said that lawyers make more money sorting out badly drawn home-made wills than they do making properly drawn wills for their clients. There is a large element of truth in this. Generally speak-ing, wills are still drawn up by solicitors for a fixed fee, which is usually a lot less than the real cost of the time involved, particularly when the responsibility factor is taken into account. In this book you will find examples of when a solicitor-drawn will is absolutely essential; for example, when you wish to protect children with learning difficulties or to set up tax-efficient trusts. In other instances, you should be able to draw up a straightforward will if you follow the guidance in the following pages. Note though that, if you are in any doubt about your circum-stances and what you wish to do, it is better to take professional advice. The heartache and expense caused by badly drawn home-made wills invariably outweighs that caused by dying without any will at all.

By professional advice I mean a solicitor and preferably one who is a member of The Society of Trust and Estate

Practitioners (STEP for short). There are numerous companies who advertise will-writing services. Quite often these are attached to companies selling insurance or financial services who are actually more interested in selling you their products than giving proper advice on your will. In essence, the low-cost will is a loss-leader. The wills produced by these companies tend to vary greatly in quality; some do produce wills of a reasonable standard but others are poorly drafted. Some of these companies do use solicitors to do the actual drafting but others don't. In fact, there is no requirement for the will-drafters to have any legal training at all. Some years ago I requested details of a franchise from a will-writing company as the firm I worked for was anxious to assess the apparent competition. It appeared that the idea was to provide a computer with a bank of clauses and hope that the basic training given enabled the will-writer to assemble a selection of clauses into a viable will. In short, standards of training and competence vary greatly and there is no easy way for the prospective customer to assess these things. Other points to look out for, if approached by one of these companies, are that they frequently charge a storage fee for keeping your will safe and will often push to have themselves made executors. There are times when professional executors are a good idea but, again, a STEP member is the better choice. This will be covered in a later chapter. Like solicitors, will-writing companies carry insurance against claims for negligent work but the value of this does depend on the company still being in existence when the time comes.

I am not planning on dying
Very few people do! Accidents happen every day of the week. If you have life assurance to protect your family in the event of your sudden death, why not make a will as well? The burden that a sudden illness or accident places on the family will be eased by a properly drawn up will specifying what you wish to happen to your effects.

There also seems to be a superstitious notion that making a will is tempting fate. This led to the Law Society producing a pamphlet entitled 'Making a will won't kill you'.

It has to be said that making a will while you are fit and healthy is far more sensible than leaving it until you are dying. It is far more distressing for the testator, the relatives and, believe it or not, the attending solicitor, if you wait until you are seriously ill in a hospital ward or hospice before deciding to make a will. The parsimonious amongst you might also note that it costs less for you to attend the solicitor's office than for him to visit you.

2

FORMALITIES FOR A WILL

Format
There is no set format for a will. With professionally drawn wills a lot depends on the individual style of the draftsman. The important thing is that the terms used are unambiguous so as to avoid costly disputes after your death. There is also no requirement for a will to be written on any special type of paper. Like a cheque it can be written on anything. For example, the London Probate Registry has a will written on an egg. However, it is not recommended that you adopt the procedure of writing on anything other than paper.

The law's requirements for a valid will are not particularly onerous.

They are:

1. The will must be in writing.
2. The document must be testamentary; that is, it is intended to take effect only on your death.
3. You must be of sound mind.
4. You must be 18 or over (21 or over before 1970).
5. The will must be executed correctly.

On the face of it, these requirements appear very easy to fulfil. In reality, there are numerous ways in which the writers of home-made wills manage to mess things up. Sometimes they omit essential matters such as the appointment of executors or write conflicting dispositions of their assets. Others simply fail to comply with the formalities of execution. I have dealt with one case where the testator wrote out the will in good style and had it witnessed by two witnesses. Unfortunately, he completely forgot to sign it himself so, as far as the law was concerned, it was of no more consequence than his shopping list.

Requirement for writing

Writing is essential. The only exception to this is where the testator is a member of the armed forces on actual military service or a mariner at sea (s. 11 Wills Act 1837). This is not an exception to rely on. It is limited in scope and intended only for use in dire emergency.

A testator may write the will in his own handwriting. This is referred to as a holograph will. Alternatively, he may type it or print it. He may even dictate it to another person to write down for him. The important thing is that it must be in writing and not, for example, recorded on tape or CD.

It is advisable to keep the writing in the will continuous. Blank pages have been accepted by the court but are best avoided. The vital thing when making your will is to ensure that you leave no scope for argument after your death. Gaps in the will may well lead to arguments that something has been left out or removed.

It is important that nothing is attached to the will by a staple, paper-clip or pin. If there are any marks indicating that something may have been attached to the will at some point, the Probate Registry will raise questions. This is because the existence of such marks suggests that perhaps a codicil or something similar was attached to the will at some stage. To avoid any such questions being raised, make sure there are no indentations, marks or small holes in the paper on which the will is written. For the same reason, avoid the use of one of those pads of paper which comes with holes already punched in it for filing purposes.

Obviously the language of a home-made will is likely to differ from that in a solicitor-drawn will. Indeed, if you insist on making your own will it is preferable not to include any legal phrases you may have come across. You may be quite confident you know what they mean but you may well be mistaken. It is best to stick to words and phrases in common parlance. Of course, the use of colloquialisms will not be seen at all in professionally drawn wills but will not render a home-made will invalid. Likewise the use of common abbreviations is acceptable for the testator writing his own document but will never be seen in a solicitor-drawn will.

It goes without saying that the writing must be legible. If your handwriting leaves a lot to be desired, it is probably best to type the will. For similar reasons it is better to avoid writing in pencil although the law does not specify that ink should be used. Remember that a will has to last a long time. If you make a will at the age of 30 it may not be proved for another 70 years or so.

Requirement for testamentary nature

The document must be clearly intended to take effect on your death. In order to be a provable will, i.e. one admissible to probate, the document must have been drawn up with what the law calls *animus testandi*. This means that whatever form the document takes, it is essential that it shows that the maker intended it to deal with the distribution of his property following his death. It is therefore important that the document can be readily distinguished from a gift intended to take effect during the maker's lifetime.

Requirement for soundness of mind

The testator must be of sound mind. He must also have full knowledge of, and approve of, the contents of the will. These points will be expanded on in a later chapter dealing with potential challenges to your will. For the moment, it may be noted that lack of knowledge and approval of the contents of a home-made will is extremely unlikely.

Contrary to popular belief a will does not usually begin with the words, 'I Fred being of sound mind and body,' nor is it usually read out at the funeral of the testator. Both these notions belong firmly in Hollywood.

Age requirement

In order to make a valid will a testator must have attained his majority. Since the coming into force of The Family Law Reform Act 1969 this is 18. The Act came into force on 1st January 1970. For wills made prior to that date, the testator had to be 21.

As previously noted, there is one exception to this rule. Under the Wills (Soldiers and Sailors) Act 1918 as amended by s. 3(1) of the Family Law Reform Act 1969, members of the armed forces in actual military service may make a will although below the age of majority.

Note that the date of execution of the will is the operative date for this rule.

Requirement for due execution

The most important thing is that the will must be executed correctly in accordance with the Wills Act 1837 as amended. This is the area where the law is most strict. Unless the will is executed properly, it is invalid and there is nothing that can be done to revive it after your death. Invalid execution is one of the most common problems with home-made wills.

The requirements for the procedure for execution are set out later in this book after we have looked at what you should put in the will. In the meantime, the following should be noted.

The will must be signed. Prior to 1st January 1983 the signature had to appear 'at the foot or end of the will'. This is no longer strictly necessary. Today the requirement is that it be apparent the 'testator intended by his signature to give effect to the will'. There are numerous cases concerning the place of signature and I will not recite the various decisions here. It will be obvious that the only safe course of action in practice is to sign the will at the end, leaving no additional words below it other than the signatures and details of the witnesses.

The will may consist of just a few lines of text or it may take up more than one sheet of paper. At one time it was a legal requirement that a will comprising several sheets must be fastened in some way so as to keep the sheets together. Over the years this rule was gradually relaxed so as to provide that holding the sheets together in the hand was sufficient. Today it would generally be accepted that if several sheets of paper concerning the disposal of property are found together they constitute the will of the deceased. To be on the safe side, it is best to staple the sheets together before signing the will.

Here a note may be added concerning the availability of numerous types of binders. Most stationery shops today will stock any number of different folders and binders for presenting documents. In the past, solicitors traditionally stitched wills together and sealed the ends of the ribbon. This remains the custom in a lot of firms today. In others binders are used. The declared preference of the Probate Registry is for wills that are not contained within plastic binders. The reason is that the original wills have to be retained by the Probate Registry and the use of bulky binders increases the space used. A staple or a paper corner will thus suffice for a home-made will. Practicality not prettiness is the rule.

It should be absolutely clear on the face of the document that it is your will. You don't want to run the risk of your relatives throwing it out as yet another piece of paper you had hoarded. A cover sheet clearly marked 'my last will' is therefore a good idea.

If your will is in several sheets it is not necessary for you to sign every page. However, you may wish to do so to indicate that nothing has been added at the foot of a page after execution of the will. This will not invalidate the will but on the final page your signature should appear only once, below the last of the writing.

Date of will

Strangely enough the law does not require a will to be dated (Corbett v Newey 1996). Following on from this it has been held that the lack of a date or inclusion of the wrong date does not invalidate a will (Corbett v Newey). If the testator thinks it is the 5th of the month and dates his will accordingly, it is not fatal to the will's validity that the actual date is the 4th. During the probate process extrinsic evidence as to the date of execution may be requested from witnesses if some doubt arises. For example, a witness may be asked to swear an affidavit explaining the circumstances in which the will was signed. The evidence is termed 'extrinsic' because it is from an outside source and not obtained from examination of the will itself.

Although a date is apparently not a strict legal require- ment, it is of great practical importance. As stated previously, the avoidance of disputes after death is the guiding principle in making the will. A clear statement as to the date of execution of the will should therefore be included. It makes no difference whether this is stated at the top of the will or at the foot of it.

Revoking a will

A will may be revoked at any time prior to the testator's death. If making a will at a solicitor's office, the solicitor will ensure that any previous will is destroyed. The making of a new will revokes the previous one by operation of law but to have old wills floating around is unsafe. Suppose the wrong one is removed from storage and taken to be your last will on your death? If you decide to make a will yourself after previously making a will with a solicitor, be sure to notify the solicitor.

Example

Mike makes a will with his solicitor when he is a 25-year- old newly wed. At the age of 45 he decides to make a few changes. He decides to do the job himself but omits to date the will or to inform his solicitor of his actions. He asks two neighbours to be witnesses. They are both elderly and die before Mike does. On his death his solicitor is holding one will and the relatives produce the handwritten one. In the absence of the witnesses a considerable argument ensues as to which is the later will. It may be that the nature of the gifts will indicate the date. For instance, if Mike refers to a house which he did not own at the time of the solicitor-made will this indicates that the home-made will is the later. On the other hand, the will may make no reference to specific gifts. An expensive argument is likely to ensue.

3

COMPONENTS OF A WILL

These are the matters you should consider before starting to write your will and which you should include in it as a minimum.

1. Your true full name.
2. Executors.
3. What the will covers.
4. Clear details of beneficiaries.
5. Funeral wishes.
6. Correct execution according to the requirements of the Wills Act 1837 as amended.

Let us consider each of these in turn.

Your details
You should state your full name and any other name by which you are commonly known. This sounds obvious but is a point often overlooked. If you have a name which can be spelt several ways it is quite possible that you have assets in more than one spelling. You may also have a middle name used only infrequently so that your bank account is in one name but your birth (and thus death) certificate says your full name. These matters can be dealt with at the probate stage but if you are commonly known by a name other than your given name it is best to include it in your will. For example, 'I John Brown otherwise known as Jack Brown'.

Executors

You will need executors. These are the people who will prove your will in the High Court via the Probate Registry, collect in your assets, settle your debts and funeral expenses and then distribute your estate to the beneficiaries. They are also responsible for safeguarding your assets during the administration period. This includes such matters as ensuring your house or other property is properly insured and protected so far as possible from risk of burglary. By the 'administration period' we mean the period between your death and the final receipts from the beneficiaries being given to the executors in exchange for their cheques. The end of the administration period is generally taken to be when the residue is ascertained. All that means in practical terms is that all liabilities are known and settled and the amount left over to pass to the beneficiaries is known. At the end of the administration period executors change hats and become known as trustees in those instances where an ongoing trust arises. If you have left money to a child, for example, they will then become responsible for investing it and looking after it until the child attains the age at which he is to receive it.

Being an executor is not an easy task. It is often time-consuming and carries a great deal of responsibility. The amount of time taken to administer an estate will, of course, vary according to how complicated the affairs of the deceased were. The number and type of assets will vary from estate to estate. Matters such as outstanding tax returns will also make a difference. Obviously a very small and straightforward estate will not take much time to sort out but the office of executor still carries legal responsibilities. For example, executors can become personally liable for your credit card bills and other debts if they do not follow correct procedures. There is a simple way to avoid this situation arising which will be explained on page 35.

It follows that you need to pick the right people for the job. They should not, for example, be people who become panicky or confused when confronted by official forms. You will need to be sure that they are honest and trustworthy and capable of understanding your instructions. It is always advisable to ask them before putting their names in your will.

Note that an executor may also benefit under your will and often a sum of money is left to an executor to recompense him for the time and trouble involved in executing the will. If you choose to do this, the gift should be expressed to apply only if the executor takes up his duties. This does not preclude you from also making your executor a beneficiary of part of your estate on top of the special legacy for proving it. If you wish your chosen executor to have a legacy, whether or not he acts as such after your death, any gift should be expressed as given 'regardless of whether he takes up his duties as executor'. A lay executor may not charge for his services but may claim out-of-pocket expenses.

Example

Mary asks Fred to be her executor. He is her favourite nephew and she is sure his experience of working in an office will enable him to do the task well. Fred agrees willingly. Mary draws up her will and leaves him a legacy of £2,000 if he takes up his duties as executor. Fred duly proves the will and handles the estate. In doing so he has to pay for death certificates from the Registrar of Births, Marriages and Deaths and incurs travelling costs arranging the funeral and clearing Mary's house. He is allowed to claim for the expenses on top of his legacy.

It may be that Mary would also wish her nephew to share in her residuary estate. If so she would leave him the £2,000 if he took up his duties as specified. She would then divide her estate between her nephew and such other beneficiaries she had in mind. If Fred were one of six nieces and nephews, for instance, he could receive one sixth of the residuary estate. Leaving him the legacy of £2,000 simply ensures he is compensated for the time and trouble he is involved in when carrying out his duties as executor.

Ideally you should appoint more than one executor to cover situations where one dies before you or is too infirm to act. The age of the executors is a factor to bear in mind. It is possible to appoint a substitute within the will.

Example
'I appoint my best friend Jim Brown to be my executor but if he predeceases me or is unable or unwilling to act I appoint my cousin Jo Baker to be executor in his place.'

It is possible to appoint your solicitor to be an executor, even if he has not drafted the will and there are advantages in doing so. Any prudent solicitor, though, will insist on reading your home-made will before placing it in his storage facility so as to ascertain that there are not likely to be any expensive and time-consuming problems arising from your drafting. Do not take offence at this. It is better to have any problems pointed out while you are still alive and able to correct them. No professional worthy of the name will insist you get the will redrawn professionally just to create an opportunity to charge you fees; if he turns pale when he reads your efforts you may be certain you have slipped up somewhere. Alternatively, you could appoint another professional, such as an accountant, as your executor although it must be said that, if your finances are complicated enough to require an accountant, you probably need a professionally drawn will.

If you decide to appoint your solicitor as executor you can also appoint a family member to act with him. This can be helpful where there is to be an ongoing trust, combining as it does professional expertise with an inside knowledge of the family's affairs. If a solicitor is appointed jointly with a family relative, then it will be expected that the solicitor will carry out the process of administering the estate. It would be very unusual indeed for a solicitor to agree to a lay person carrying out the administration on his behalf. Indeed, there would almost certainly be implications with regard to his professional negligence insurance if he did. If your estate has dwindled by the time of your death so that there is very little to be sorted out, the solicitor will usually renounce probate, i.e. sign a document for the Probate Registry stating that he declines to take up his duties as executor. The other executor may then continue alone. Even where there is a sizeable estate the solicitor executor may choose to renounce if asked to do so but is not obliged to do so. It is generally felt within the solicitors' profession that where a client appoints a solicitor as executor he did so for a reason and accepted that the solicitor would charge for the administration. It is, in my experience, very common for a client to express a view as to his relatives' behaviour after his death which is proved to be all too correct. This applies not only to his choice of beneficiaries but to his choice of executors as well. A lay executor may also renounce if he doesn't feel able to take up his duties. Sometimes a will contains an appointment of another person as executor in substitution if one executor is unable or unwilling to take up his duties.

An alternative step to renunciation by an executor is the 'power reserved' option. This means that one executor takes out the Grant of Probate in his sole name but it is marked 'power reserved' to the other executor. This means that the other executor can take out a Grant of Probate in his own right at a later date if he wishes. In contrast, an executor who renounces does so once and for all.

Why have professional executors?
The term 'professional executor' means an executor who is paid to act as such. The term includes solicitors, accountants and the trust departments of banks. There are often advantages in having a professional executor, particularly where the estate is large and/or complicated or there are ongoing trusts to administer. Professionals are not emotionally involved and the importance of this

should not be underestimated. In the immediate after-math of a death people go through a range of emotions including guilt, disbelief, anger and denial. All of these may be experienced in one degree or another depending on the closeness of the relationship and the circumstances of the death. Occasionally, the bereaved relatives may feel unable to deal with things because of the memories involved or may themselves be ill and unable to deal with matters. Consider, for example, the situation where a person is killed in a car crash and his spouse is seriously injured. There may be a pressing need to deal with household bills, etc., or to arrange accommodation and funding for small children. Having a professional executor can be a godsend in such circumstances.

I have experienced several situations where the executor, being a close relative of the deceased, refused to give instructions or talk about the deceased for a long time after the death because it was too painful. Although creditors such as credit card companies understand the need for probate and so on they are unlikely to be sympathetic to a lengthy delay in sorting matters out because the lay executor cannot face dealing with them. Even being ill and hospitalised is unlikely to buy you much extra time.

Another advantage of emotional detachment is that professional executors can sit back from family disputes. If you think there is any chance of your family not liking what you have written in your will, appoint at least one professional executor. It may be that you have two children who have never seen eye to eye. Appointing one or other as executor is a recipe for disaster and appointing both probably not much better. It is not uncommon for a bemused solicitor to find himself bombarded with letters and phone calls from warring factions in the family, both telling him how despicable the other party is.

Professional executors will be well versed in the relevant law and practice of estate administration. If you have used words that are ambiguous or have used legal terms incorrectly a lay executor may misinterpret your wishes. Indeed

I wonder how many times wills have been administered incorrectly due to a failure to understand the words used. This applies both to home-made wills and to where a lay executor insists on administering an estate himself using a solicitor-drawn will.

There are time-limits to be observed for certain steps of the administration and many a lay executor has been caught out. Tax can also be a cause of major headaches for the lay executor. If your estate is over the inheritance tax threshold by more than a few pounds it is probably unlikely a lay executor can cope without professional assistance. Where tax is concerned, this need not be a solicitor of course. A lay executor might consult an accountant for assistance with tax calculations or completion of income tax returns instead.

If the estate is complicated because you have foreign shares, a holiday home abroad or wish to create an ongoing trust, the burden on a lay executor will be enormous. Suppose you die when your child is a year old. The trust would last at least 17 years, probably longer if you have specified that the money is to be paid over at an age later than 18. Do you really wish to burden a relative for that period? The duty of care on trustees is so onerous, particularly since the coming into force of The Trustee Act 2000, that it is scarcely reasonable to burden a lay person with the office for over twenty years.

Another reason for professional trustees, which sadly is becoming more and more important in these increasingly litigious times, is that they carry insurance. They are also subject to the rules and disciplinary procedures of their profession. If a lay executor runs off with the money intended for the beneficiaries there is in reality little the beneficiaries can do. Criminal proceedings may follow, compensation may be awarded but whether it will be paid is another matter. Professional executors carry insurance in case they make a mistake (professional negligence) and solicitors have a compensation scheme where theft has occurred.

If you have an ongoing relationship with a firm of solicitors, you may feel happier leaving your affairs in the hands of someone you already know and trust. You have the choice of appointing the firm itself (in reality, the partners at the time of your death) or a named solicitor within it.

Banks will also act as executors but their charges are generally much higher than those charged by solicitors. Your bank can give you details of its current charges but (as with solicitors' charges) the charges at the time of your death may well be higher. It is always the scale in force at the date of death that applies. If you appoint your bank, the work will be handled by whichever member of their staff in the executor and trustee department is available at the time. It is not possible to appoint an individual staff member as it is with a solicitor. Banks may also renounce probate if requested to do so or the estate turns out to be too small to warrant their involvement.

Professional help for lay executors
If you name a lay executor in your will, he can always select a solicitor to administer your estate on his behalf. Most solicitors' firms have a wills and probate department; and he would be well advised to choose a member of the Society of Trust and Estate Practitioners.

The solicitor will obtain the figures to go in the probate papers, draw up the application and arrange for the executor to sign it. All correspondence will be dealt with by the solicitor who will forward withdrawal forms, stock transfer forms, etc., to the executor. At the end of the administration a set of accounts will be drawn up for the executor's approval before cheques are sent out to the beneficiaries. The solicitor's fees will be deducted from the estate as a testamentary expense.

As with the drafting of wills, there are companies who advertise that they specialise in estate administration. Such companies are not solicitors although they may employ solicitors in-house or retain the services of outside firms when necessary. They are not covered by the regulations of The Law Society and there is little redress if something goes wrong. There have been several instances of such companies going into liquidation with the result that the beneficiaries lost all their money. It is better to avoid such companies.

What happens if no executors are appointed?
If you fail to appoint executors this does not affect the validity of your will but does mean that a Grant of Probate will not be issued. Instead, one of the beneficiaries will need to make application for a Grant of Letters of Administration with the Will Annexed. There is a set order of entitlement to such a grant. The person who is entitled to the residue of the estate (i.e. the person who has been left the remains of the estate after the payment of all charges, debts and bequests) has the prior entitlement. The practical effect is that you may end up with your estate being administered by someone who would not have been your first choice. The same applies if you appoint an executor who dies before you or is unable to take up his duties.

The administration of your estate is dealt with in exactly the same way, regardless of which type of grant is issued, but there is a practical difference between executors and administrators. This is that an executor takes his authority from the will and can act before the Grant of Probate issues. In contrast, an administrator takes his authority from the Grant of Letters of Administration and cannot act before he receives it. This difference enables an executor to collect in smaller assets by producing a copy of the will before he receives the grant, subject, of course, to the rules of the asset-holder concerned.

What the will is intended to cover
As a general rule, a will executed in England and Wales covers all your immoveable property (houses, for instance) within the jurisdiction and moveable property anywhere in

the world (bank accounts, for example). It is possible to make more than one will specifying the limitations of each, e.g. 'This will is intended to relate only to my affairs in England and Wales.' If you have a property in Spain you will almost certainly need another will to cover it. You also need to be aware that the requirements for release of the funds differ from one country to another. In some countries the concept of executors is unknown.

If you have assets in two different countries and attempt to make two wills there is the danger of accidentally revoking an English will by a foreign will and vice versa. Such matters are outside the intended scope of this book. If you have assets in another country seek specialist advice, do not attempt to make your own will.

A common mistake made by writers of home-made wills is that they believe they have to state all their assets in the will. For example:

'I give my bank account with H bank no. 1234, my building society account with D building society no. 3456, my shares in British Gas, my bicycle, my furniture, my car and the cash in my piggy bank to my wife.'

The problems likely to arise are that you may have closed the accounts during your lifetime and you may have changed your mode of transport.

Let us say you have a bank account no. 1234 at the time you write this in your will. During your lifetime you discover that a better rate of interest is available if you switch to another account. Being a sensible investor you switch accounts. When you die, the law will not say, 'Oh he changed account no. 1234 to account no. 4567.' It will say, 'Account no. 1234 was closed and thus his wife does not receive the money it once contained.' A partial intestacy may follow unless you have gone on to say that you leave all your other assets to your children, for instance. It is important to avoid a partial intestacy arising if you want to know exactly where your money will end up. If the gifts in the will do not use up all your assets then anything left over will pass according to the intestacy rules. This situation is what is meant by a partial intestacy and is usually brought about by a testator acquiring assets after the date of the will but not having inserted a general gift of residue (i.e. not specifying who is to inherit the remainder of his estate).

If you wish to give everything to one person simply say so. Examples of simple wills are given at the back of this book but, briefly, you can say, 'After payment of all liabilities I give everything I own to my wife.'

Types of gifts

Gifts in a will are referred to as legacies. There are a number of different types.

SPECIFIC LEGACIES

It is possible to gift a particular asset to a certain person. For instance, you may wish to leave your car to your son. If so, it should be clearly stated. For example, 'I give my Mercedes registration no. ABC 123 to my son Fred.' Likewise you can leave the money in a designated account by stating, 'I give the money standing to the credit of my account no. 1234 at XYZ bank to my niece Jane.'

Note that if it is likely you will change a specified asset such as a car during your lifetime it is far better to say, 'I give any car which I own at my death to my son.'

Such a gift is known as a specific legacy. If the car has been sold during your lifetime, the intended recipient will receive nothing.

The costs of transferring such a gift to the beneficiary are borne by the beneficiary unless you specify otherwise. To avoid this you should state the gift to be 'free of costs of delivery'. If you leave a house to one beneficiary, then the costs of insuring it and transferring it to him will be payable by him unless you specify otherwise. It is also important to specify whether or not your estate is to be responsible for paying off any remaining mortgage on the property.

Sometimes when a beneficiary receives a valuable specific legacy, the gift is stated to bear its own tax. The general rule is that inheritance tax is payable out of residue. If the testator feels that a particularly valuable gift should bear its own tax, the words 'and I direct that this gift shall bear its own tax in exoneration of my residuary estate' should be used.

MONETARY LEGACIES

If you wish to leave a sum of money to a friend or relative, this is known as a pecuniary legacy. You can express this simply: 'I give the sum of £3,000 to my friend Paul Smith.' You may wish to add a few words to express the reason for the gift, e.g. 'in recognition of his kindness to me during my lifetime.' Perhaps you have been a member of a social club and wish the members to hold an event in memory of your times together. In those circumstances say, 'I give the sum of £3,000 to the Anytown Thursday Social Club with the request that they hold a dinner for the members in my memory.' It is of great assistance to your executors to add the full address of your friend or the organiser of your social club.

If you wish to leave a pecuniary legacy to a child, special rules apply. If the child is very young, you will be faced with the problem that he cannot give a valid receipt to the executors. The law says that a child under 18 cannot give a receipt for a legacy. To get round this, you may specify that the executors may accept a receipt from his parents or you may specify that he does not receive the money until he is 18 or older.

Unless a pecuniary legacy is given to your own child or is expressed to be for the child's immediate maintenance, it does not carry interest. Let us say you leave £5,000 to your nephew on attaining the age of 18 years. He is six when you die. He cannot have the £5,000 until he is 18 but he cannot have any interest gained from investing it either (which belongs to the residuary beneficiary). When he is 18 he will receive £5,000 and nothing more. The way round this is to specify that the gift is to carry the intermediate income.

If you wish the gift to be given to the child's parents it is important to protect your executors by giving them authority to accept a receipt and to say that they are not liable for seeing how the money is spent. You do not want the child to come back to your executors many years later and complain that they gave his money to his parents who promptly spent it on a foreign holiday.

A pecuniary legacy may also be referred to as a general legacy.

DEMONSTRATIVE LEGACIES

A demonstrative legacy is a pecuniary legacy payable out of a particular fund. For instance, you may wish a beneficiary to receive half of the proceeds from an insurance policy. You may wish a sum of money to be paid from a certain bank account.

Liabilities

Again, it is not necessary to list your debts. All debts owed at the time of your death will be offset against your assets. For instance, your credit card bills and utility bills will be paid before your estate is distributed to your beneficiaries. It may be very helpful to your executors to leave a list of liabilities and assets with the will so they know what they are dealing with. You can update this from time to time. A specimen form of assets/liabilities log appears on page 129.

If your executors are wise they will insert a notice to creditors in accordance with section 27 of The Trustee Act 1925. This goes in the *London Gazette* and a newspaper circulating in the district in which you last resided. The notice gives creditors two months to notify the executors of their claim against the estate. Failure to insert such a notice will leave the executors open to personal liability if they are notified of a debt after distributing the estate.

Beneficiaries

It is very, very important to be absolutely clear to whom you are referring in your will. Remember that your executors will not have the same knowledge of your affairs as you do. Even close family members may hold different opinions on the family relationships.

Expressions to avoid include 'my favourite nephew' (without naming him), 'my best friend' (again without naming him), 'the girl who brings round the tea' (an actual example from my experience), 'the man next door'.

It is also highly desirable to avoid nicknames. In one famous case the testator stated 'all to mother' because he called his wife 'mother'. Although this was accepted in court and the wife received everything, the court action could have been avoided entirely by avoiding the nickname.

If you have a pet name for one of your children it is best to avoid using this in the will. For example, I knew someone who always referred to his son as 'The little fella' which expression would have been most unfortunate to use in his will. Suppose, for example, he had gone on to develop a close friendship with somebody who was of very small build? In the event of a dispute, evidence may be accepted by the court so as to prove the use of the name but a lot of money will be taken up by the litigation. If you have only one daughter but two sons and wish to use a pet name for your daughter, then you should at least state that she is your daughter. For example, 'I give my entire estate to my sons Bill and Ben and my daughter the princess in equal shares.'

It is very important to name any beneficiary who is not actually a blood relative. Stepchildren are not included in the description 'my children' but legally adopted children are. If you have been married for many years and regard your spouse's children as your own, it is easy to forget that the law sees things differently. If you do not wish to point out the fact that one child is a stepchild, you should simply name all of them rather than using the phrase 'my children'. In fact, it is better specifically to name them anyway as this will assist your executors in identifying the recipients of your estate. It must always be borne in mind that family quarrels and breakdowns can occur. On your death the size of your family may not always be apparent, particularly to a professional executor. Naming your children individually ensures that your executors are aware of their existence, even if their whereabouts is not immediately known.

It should be mentioned that there is one drawback to naming your children individually in your will. The birth of your first child is one of the occasions when you should consider revising your will or making a will if you haven't already done so. If you are likely to increase your family in the future then you will have to make a fresh will to include the new child each time.

Addresses are of great assistance to executors but are not legally essential. The important thing is that there is no room for doubt as to whom the will is intended to benefit. If you do insert addresses make sure they are correct. Half-remembered or out-of-date addresses can create more problems than having no addresses at all. It is not necessary to make a fresh will just because addresses change. If you or a beneficiary changes address following execution of your will, you should place an explanatory piece of paper in the envelope with it. Do not change the address on the will itself.

Residuary estate

The term 'residuary estate' or 'residue' refers to everything left over after you have paid your debts and the costs of administering your estate and given any specific or pecuniary legacies. It includes everything else you own. Usually you will be giving this to one person such as your spouse or to a group of people such as your children.

At its most simple the will could say, 'I give everything else I own to my wife.' Your wife will then receive everything left over after paying the liabilities and specific and pecuniary legacies.

A better way of expressing it is to say, 'After payment of my just debts, funeral and testamentary expenses and the legacies given by this will I leave all the rest of my property of whatever kind to my wife.'

It is important that you dispose of your entire estate correctly. If you make errors so as to leave some part of your estate undisposed of, a partial intestacy will arise. This means that the legacies in your will take effect but the undisposed of part goes to whoever would inherit your estate under the intestacy rules.

Death of a beneficiary

You must consider the possibility of a beneficiary dying before you or with you in what the law refers to as 'a common accident'. In addition, there is always the chance that your intended beneficiary will be charged with your murder and thus be prevented from inheriting. Divorce also raises issues as we shall see in Chapter 5.

In a typical situation a couple will leave everything to each other on the first death and everything to the children on the second death.

To cater for this, the will should state that, 'If my wife dies before me or the gift to her fails for any other reason I give my estate after settlement of liabilities to such of my children who are alive at my death and if more than one in equal shares.'

If a dead beneficiary has been left a specific or pecuniary legacy the gift will usually fall into residue unless you have specified that it is to go to somebody else in that event. Note that if a beneficiary survives you by even a few hours his estate receives the legacy unless you state otherwise.

Beware of using phrases such as 'to my wife and after her death' as this may be interpreted as giving your wife a life interest only. A life interest is where the beneficiary receives the income from the investment of the capital fund but the capital fund is destined for another beneficiary on the death of the life tenant. Home-made wills frequently include gifts to this effect, the intention quite often being to indicate that if the wife has predeceased, the children, for example, receive the estate instead. Since the coming into force of The Administration of Justice Act 1982 there is now a presumption that the gift to the spouse is intended to be absolute unless the will indicates otherwise (s. 22).

Survivorship clauses
To cater for the possibility of two deaths occurring simultaneously or very close together, some people choose to insert a survivorship clause. The period usually chosen is 28 days or a calendar month but can be up to six months. Such a provision can prevent your money ending up where you did not intend it to go.

EXAMPLE
Jim makes a will leaving everything to his best friend Paul. They have known each other since school and have been firm friends for more years than either of them wishes to think about. Jim has never married and has no relatives to whom he feels any obligation. Paul is married but his wife does not like Jim very much. Jim has always thought that Paul's wife is jealous of their friendship and he tends not to visit the house when she is there. One day Jim and Paul are driving to a race meeting together when an accident occurs. Jim dies instantly but Paul makes it to hospital where he dies several hours later. Jim's will does not include a survivorship clause so his money and goods pass to Paul. Under the terms of Paul's will everything goes to his wife. Paul's wife thus inherits everything Paul owned as well as everything Jim owned. If Jim had specified that Paul had to survive him by one month this result would have been avoided.

In this example Jim would, of course, have had to specify a recipient of his estate if Paul did not survive him by the specified period. He could, perhaps, have left his estate to a favourite charity or to another friend.

DISADVANTAGES OF A SURVIVORSHIP CLAUSE

The most obvious disadvantage is the need to wait for the funds. A widow may have a real need for immediate funds on her husband's death and a survivorship clause will increase the waiting period. As an aside it bears noting that it is advisable for married couples to have one account in joint names so that funds will be accessible to the survivor regardless of the probate process. Probate can often be a drawn out process in any event and the existence of an emergency fund can be of great value.

If husband and wife die in circumstances where their estates may be subject to inheritance tax, a survivorship clause may also be a disadvantage. This is due to the interaction of two different statutory provisions and is something on which professional advice is required.

Funeral wishes

You should always make your funeral wishes known to your family as your will may not be found and opened until after it has taken place. However, there are still good reasons to refer to your funeral wishes in the will itself, especially if they are out of the ordinary. If your family are aware you left a will they will undoubtedly check the will for funeral wishes. If your funeral needs to be arranged by your solicitor or by someone other than a close family member, directions in the will can be very helpful. The person arranging the funeral will want to know that he is doing what you would have wished. The most basic choice is between burial and cremation. If you do not specify which you want, the chances are that the person arranging the funeral will do what he would choose for himself. Remember that at a time when they are emotionally distressed your family will not need the additional stress of wondering whether they have done what you would have wished.

You should at the very minimum specify your choice between burial and cremation. Some people go a lot further and specify the Bible readings and hymns they wish to have. Sometimes they desire there to be no dark clothes or flowers.

The law says that the funeral expenses are a charge on your estate. It is usually expected that your funeral will be arranged according to your station in life. A solicitor executor will have to be sure the amount expended is reasonable in relation to your estate so as to avoid allegations of overspending from the beneficiaries. It is therefore important that if you want a big funeral or a particular item such as a horse-drawn hearse, a jazz band or a Scottish piper, you specify this in the will so as to authorise your executors to pay for it.

A memorial is not a testamentary expense even though it is now a deductible expense for inheritance tax purposes. If you wish to have a memorial paid for from your estate you must say so. This is especially important if you are leaving your estate to charity, for example. Family members may not object to money being spent on a memorial but to avoid arguments give your executors the power to pay for it.

Clarity is everything

In setting out your wishes the guiding principle is clarity. This point cannot be stressed enough.

Punctuation, if used at all, needs careful attention. In professionally drawn wills in the past, punctuation was never used. Today some professional wills do include punctuation but much depends on the style of the draftsman. In a home-made will any punctuation should be used very carefully. At the time of writing I am dealing with a home-made will where no executor was appointed. The question of who is entitled to a Grant of Letters of Administration with the Will Annexed turns on the construction of the testamentary gifts and the answer is by no means clear. The gifts include gifts of assets that no longer exist and the last paragraph of the will is ambiguous. There are two faint marks in the text which appear to be

full stops but might be accidental blots of ink. The outcome of the case will depend on the interpretation placed
upon those marks.

The important thing to bear in mind is that the will
must work when viewed in isolation, that is to say, without
the benefit of inside knowledge of the testator's affairs or
evidence of such from a witness. Once you have finished
your will, leave it for 24 hours then return to it, read it and
ask yourself, 'Would a complete stranger reading this
understand what I mean?' Be absolutely honest with yourself and only proceed further when you are satisfied that
the answer is 'Yes.' Even better, get a trusted friend to read
it and tell you what he thinks it means. Compare what he
says to what you intended and amend your writing accordingly.

Execution of the will
This is the most important thing of all. Unless you adhere
strictly to the procedure required by law your will is
invalid. This is the area where a lot of home-made wills
come to grief.

The Wills Act 1837 as amended requires the following:
Two witnesses must be in the room when you sign the will.
They must see you sign the will and they must then sign
the will in your presence and in the presence of each other.
All three of you must remain in the room throughout the
entire procedure. The will must be signed with your usual
signature. A testator who cannot write may make a mark
such as a cross on the paper but the fact that it was signed
by a mark must be stated in the attestation clause. If it is a
lengthy will it is advisable to sign the bottom of each page
so as to show that nothing has been added after you signed
it. If you spot any errors when you come to sign the will,
initial them and get the witnesses to do the same. Do not
change anything after the will has been executed.

The will should also be dated so as to avoid any
arguments later.

The witnesses should print their names after their signatures and add their names, addresses and occupations. It is not necessary for the witnesses to read the will but they must be told that they are witnessing your will in case they are later required to give evidence. This point is most important. There is no point having two witnesses if you do not make it plain to them that you are signing your will.

The importance of this last point was clearly demonstrated in the recent case of In Re the Estate of Richard Sherrington. In that case Mr Sherrington's stepdaughter, who had no legal training or qualifications, prepared a will for him. He signed the will in his office on an evening when he was in a hurry to catch a plane. He asked two people to witness his signature and they duly signed their names as he directed. When he died his children disputed that the will, which left everything to his second wife with whom he was apparently not on very good terms, was correctly executed. On the face of it, the will had been executed correctly. However, the evidence revealed that one witness did not realise that 'anything important had taken place' on that evening and the other witness spoke very little English. Both gave evidence to the effect that they had not seen the deceased sign the will and when they signed had no intention of verifying or attesting the deceased's signature. The will was declared invalid as a result of the failure to observe the correct procedure for executing it.

Who may be a witness?
Anyone may be a witness unless he is blind. There is no minimum age requirement but obviously common sense must be applied. The witnesses may be called to give evidence after your death and should therefore be of a suitable age and competent to give evidence. Although the law does not require a witness to be over 18 it is probably preferable for this to be so. For practical reasons it may be best to seek out witnesses somewhat younger than you.

The point of having witnesses is so that they can speak after your death if queries arise.

A beneficiary should not witness the will since a witness cannot benefit from a will he has witnessed. Note that if a beneficiary witnesses the will or is married to a witness, the gift to him is void. The will is still valid but the witnessing beneficiary does not receive his gift. It does not matter if a witness later marries a beneficiary; it is the situation at the date of the will that matters.

An executor may witness the will but should not do so if you are leaving him a legacy for his trouble. He will not appreciate doing all the work and then being denied his gift for the reasons given above.

On the basis that it is better to be safe than sorry, choose as your witnesses people who are not mentioned in the will at all. There is no objection to a married couple acting as witnesses as long as neither receives a gift in the will.

It may be wondered how anyone would ever know if the strict formalities for execution of the will were not adhered to but these things have a way of coming to light. I dealt with a case two years ago where the testatrix had obviously started to write 'May' in the will and changed it to 'June'. Given that the will was dated the third of the month this seemed understandable enough, the testatrix having possibly momentarily forgotten that the month had changed. The Probate Registry asked for an affidavit of due execution to be sworn by the witnesses so as to be sure the formalities had been complied with. The witnesses were duly approached and asked if they would swear a document stating they had been present and seen the testatrix sign her will. Both of them telephoned me and were most helpful and willing to co-operate. Unfortunately, they both told me that they had never met each other. It transpired that the testatrix had asked one witness to witness her signature and asked the other on a later date. The will was thus invalid.

There have been numerous cases where the attestation of the will has been brought into question. Many of these involve the position of the testator and witnesses within the room and whether such behaviour as the testator or witnesses peeping through doorways and windows to see each other sign amounts to due execution. Why a testator should approach the signing of such an important document in such a bizarre way is a matter for conjecture. It is certainly not recommended that such a cavalier approach be adopted.

Caution is advised if you decide to sign your will at a family reunion or some such event. If you must do this, try to avoid picking two witnesses who live at opposite ends of the country. There are dicta to the effect that this arouses a suspicion that the two witnesses were not present at the same time ('dicta' being comments made by a judge in the course of delivering his judgment). The result is that the Probate Registry may ask for an affidavit of due execution when the will is sent to them. Certainly a solicitor receiving such a document back from a testator is expected to make enquiry of his client as to whether the witnesses were present together with the testator when they signed. In fact the recommended procedure for solicitors is that they require their clients to attend the office to execute their wills. I can testify from experience that this saves a lot of time and trouble.

4

WHAT PROPERTY CAN YOU LEAVE BY WILL?

You can include in your will anything and everything owned in your sole name within England and Wales. You can also include money in foreign bank accounts but land in other countries is a different matter. Special rules apply to foreign real estate and advice from a lawyer well versed in the law of the country in question is essential.

When writing your will, it is important to bear in mind that a lot of things can change between the date of your will and your death. It will be construed as if you had signed it as your very last act before dying no matter how many years have elapsed in reality since you signed it. However, this rule does not apply to a description of some specific thing in existence at the date of the will. This is why you must be careful about the descriptions of property used in the will.

The man who writes his own will usually does so confident in the knowledge that on his death it will be obvious what he meant. He fondly imagines that common sense will apply and that everyone will understand his intentions. That this is far from the case with the majority of home-made wills is something which bears repeating. If the estate is a large one the sum of money at stake can be significant. If the estate is small the legal fees for sorting it out may well erode most of the benefit to the winner. Time and again the testator's common-sense provisions end up in the courts for construction. The case law on the interpretation of wills is enormous. It seems that at some time or another almost every word a testator can use to describe something he owns or wishes to do has been subjected to the court's scrutiny. It is not proposed to go over this here other than to mention one or two of the more common phrases that seem to trip up the makers of home-made wills.

Houses

If you own your house in your sole name then you can leave it as a specific gift to someone. If you still have a mortgage on it, then it is vital to specify that you intend the mortgage to be paid off out of the rest of your estate. If you intend the beneficiary to sell it to redeem the mortgage or to go on paying it from his own funds, you must state the gift to be 'subject to any mortgage thereon'. Avoid stating the address of the property in case you move during your lifetime. However, it is in order to say, 'My house no. 3 Acacia Gardens or such house as I have purchased in substitution therefore during my lifetime.'

If you also own a holiday home, take care to specify which of the two properties you intend to gift. In addition you need to bear in mind that overseas property may be subject to different rules. If you own a holiday home in France or Spain, you will almost certainly need a separate will and you will need to take specialist advice.

Timeshare properties are another difficult area. These will often be owned by a company based somewhere like the Isle of Man and the timeshare owners then have shares in the company. The mechanism of succession will usually have been discussed at the time of purchase but forgotten by the time the will is made. If you own the right to stay in a villa in Spain for two weeks each year, a gift of 'my villa in Spain' will almost certainly not work.

Contents

You may wish the recipient of your house to have the contents as well. You may think this simple enough but what does 'contents' mean in this context? According to the decided cases the contents of a house include every-thing that a tenant would be entitled to remove from a house he rented. In one case the furniture stored in the detached garage was deemed not to be included in the gift of the house and contents. Should you decide just to leave a piece of furniture to a friend, remember to specify whether the contents pass as well. For example, if you have a desk at home you can gift this with or without the contents. As the contents will include any sums of money you have left in the desk drawer be careful as to what you specify and where you hide your nest egg. When leaving legacies of heavy items it is important to state whether the recipient is to pay the costs of delivery or whether your estate is to do so. In the absence of directions, the recipient bears all the costs.

Jewellery
Most women, and increasingly a lot of men, have items of jewellery such as rings that they wish to pass to specific beneficiaries. Again, this may seem a simple word but what does it cover? Clearly it covers diamond necklaces, ear-rings and wedding rings but is a watch to be included? An eighteenth century case reached the conclusion that it wasn't but whether that would necessarily apply today is debatable. Is a watch just a practical item or is it for adornment? It might well be argued that a watch is now a fashion item in many instances; certainly it can be a status symbol. Suppose you mounted a coin or something similar into a ring or a necklace? Does a shark's tooth on a lanyard count? It would appear that 'personal jewellery' may be construed as meaning only those items used or worn personally by the deceased. If so, where does the current fashion for nose studs and other body piercing leave us? Are these to be considered items of jewellery and would anyone actually appreciate being bequeathed them? It may be best to leave a list of specific items in the will or, perhaps, to leave your jewellery box and the entire contents to one person.

If you decide to leave your jewellery box and contents to be divided between your daughters you should add that the decision of your executors as to who receives what is final and binding on all parties. If you wish the division to result in all parties receiving items to approximately the same value you should say so.

Money

This is a word of which the writers of home-made wills seem especially fond in my experience – we all know what the word means, don't we? Well, once the lawyers fall to debating it, things can be different from what they seem at first glance. In fact, the word does not have a definite technical meaning. Should your will end up in court a lot will depend on how the lawyers read the word in the context of your will and overall circumstances. Over the years it has been held to include cash, banknotes and money in your current account. On the other hand, it would appear that the judges consider that it does not include money in a deposit account where a long notice period prior to withdrawal is required. It does not include stocks and shares. The best advice one can give the testator is to avoid the use of the word 'money' completely.

In one home-made will I dealt with an elderly woman had not seen her son for many years. She did not wish him to receive a single penny because of the way he had treated her. Unfortunately, she chose to leave her 'money' to a friend. Due to the case law referred to above, only part of her estate went to her friend. Those accounts that did not come within the decided cases on the definition of money were subject to a partial intestacy and passed to her son.

Investments

From a perusal of the decided cases it would seem that this word covers stock market based investments but not money held in a deposit account. It might well be that this construction sits quite well with the layman's understanding of the word even if puzzling for the lawyers. Again, try to avoid using it if possible.

Car

You probably change your car from time to time, either through necessity or a desire to keep up with the Joneses. If you wish someone to benefit from your car on your death, the safest thing is to say 'any car which I may own at my death'. Care needs to be taken though if you own more than one car and the other is used by your spouse or child. He or she may not appreciate a beneficiary making a claim on it. This could make things a little difficult when writing your will. You will need to be precise as to the car intended to pass. Perhaps it is best to say, 'my Mercedes registration no. 123 XYZ or any car which I may have purchased in substitution therefore during my lifetime.'

Take care also if you have one vehicle for business use and one for personal use.

Business

If you run your own business don't make your own will. There are too many problems likely to arise without professional help. For example, if your business is run from office premises does the gift of the business include the premises? Does it carry the goodwill and the stock? What if you are in partnership and you have a partnership deed that conflicts with your will? It may be a long time since you read the agreement with your partners. It may not say what you remember it saying. Note that you cannot force your partners to take on a particular person as a partner, so don't try to leave them a new partner in your will.

Business assets attract special relief for inheritance tax purposes. This in itself can create problems in drawing up a will. For example, if you have a will drawn up by a solicitor and it incorporates a nil rate band discretionary trust, great care is needed to ensure that the trust doesn't end up with far more than the testator intended. For advice on leaving business assets, see a solicitor or accountant.

Chattels

There have been various decisions as to what is meant by 'chattels', 'personal effects' and 'personal goods.' This is one instance where you might consider making an exception to the golden rule of not using legal phrases in a home-made will. The word 'chattels' is defined in s. 55(1)(x) of The Administration of Estates Act 1925 for the purposes of the intestacy rules. If asked to include a gift of chattels most solicitors will adopt the statutory definition in a will. You can incorporate this by simply stating, 'I give to my son my personal chattels as defined by s. 55(1)(x) of The Administration of Estates Act 1925.'

The definition is as follows:

'carriages, horses, stable furniture and effects (not used for business purposes), motor cars and accessories (not used for business purposes), garden effects, domestic animals, plate, plated articles, linen, china, glass, books, pictures, prints, furniture, jewellery, articles of household or personal use or ornament, musical and scientific instruments and apparatus, wines, liquors and consumable stores, but do not include any chattels used at the death of the intestate for business purposes nor money or securities for money'.

This definition may seem a little old-fashioned but it will do the job.

Royalties

If you write a best-selling novel you will be entitled to royalties from the publication. These will continue for the period of copyright and may be bequeathed to your heirs. The most well-known example of this is the rights to *Peter Pan* which were bequeathed to Great Ormond Street Hospital for Sick Children. If you are a really famous author you may well need to appoint separate executors known as literary executors, to deal with royalties from your books. In that event you almost certainly have a tax problem as well and require expert advice.

Joint property

One big mistake frequently encountered in home-made wills is that the testator thinks he can leave his half of the house to his children rather than his wife. This is probably the area where the gap between the reality of the legal situation and the understanding of the common man is widest.

It is probably true to say that most married couples would regard themselves as owning half a house each. Nowadays it is fairly rare to come across the situation where the house belongs to the husband alone. Couples today buy the house together with a joint mortgage and regard themselves as equal owners. Most are surprised to discover that the law regards them as owning their house under a trust arrangement and that they are regarded as trustees.

For the purposes of the law there are two different estates held by co-owners, one is the legal estate and the other the equitable (beneficial) estate. It is the equitable estate that may be varied to suit the circumstances of the testator. There are two ways of holding the equitable estate, these are known as a joint tenancy and a tenancy in common.

Joint tenancy

Under a joint tenancy the property passes by survivorship and not through the will. This is the most common arrangement encountered amongst married couples. On the death of one, the house becomes the sole property of the other and this is what the majority of couples would consider their wishes to be. However, there can be a situation where the surviving spouse owning the house outright is undesirable for tax reasons in particular. It is then preferable to hold the house as tenants in common.

Tenants in common

When a house is owned by two or more people as tenants in common each of them has a separate interest he can leave in his will. This arrangement is useful where there are tax considerations or where there has been a prior marriage. For example, it may be desired to protect the children from a prior marriage against the risk of being disinherited by the second spouse. This will be covered in more detail in the next chapter.

It is possible to change the ownership of a house from a joint tenancy to a tenancy in common. This involves drawing up a special form of notice, serving it on the other co-owner and then registering a restriction at the Land Registry. If you are in a situation where a severance is necessary it is highly likely your affairs are too complicated to attempt your own will.

It is essential to note that unless you own your property as tenants in common neither you nor your co-owner can leave your share to anybody else. The will cannot override the survivorship that occurs on death. Any purported gift of the property will be void. This can lead to great disappointment on the part of the named recipient and may also cause hardship.

If you do not know how you hold the property it is very likely that you own as joint tenants. In the absence of specific instructions to the contrary most property lawyers would register a married couple as joint tenants. You can confirm this by obtaining office copies of your title from the Land Registry. If you own as tenants in common there will be a restriction recorded to the effect that the survivor cannot give a valid receipt for capital monies without an order of the registrar or of the court. This will appear after your names on the proprietorship register. If no such words appear then you hold as joint tenants. Your title number will appear on your title document. If you do not have this you can do a search of the Index Map at the Land Registry to obtain it. The Index Map Search is free but there is a charge for the office copies. The charges are increased periodically. To find your nearest Land Registry, consult the telephone directory or go to their website.

5

WHO MAY BENEFIT FROM A WILL?

As we shall see there are very few people who cannot benefit from your will but the way you describe the recipients of your estate is important. In describing people in your will the same caveats apply as with describing your assets. Clarity is the order of the day.

Children

Obviously the children of your marriage can benefit from your will and your spouse's will. Indeed they will be entitled to complain if you omit to mention them. Stepchildren need to be specifically named if you wish to benefit them. The law does not regard them as entitled to anything as of right so they will not be included in a gift referring to your children.

It may be that you live with someone without being married to him or her. Perhaps you both had children before you met and both sets of children live with you. To complicate matters further you may have gone on to have other children together.

If you make a will stating that you leave everything to your children only your own children will fall within the definition 'my children'. In the scenario above these would include the subsequent children but not your other half's children from a previous relationship. Even if you have married, your stepchildren will not be included as your children. If you have lived with them for a long time you may well regard them as your own children to all intents and purposes. It is therefore easy to overlook the need specifically to name all children other than your own. In any event, it is far better to name all your children rather than to use a generic description. This ensures that the executors are aware of the existence of all of them. I have dealt with more than one case where a child attempted to conceal a parent's death from a brother or sister.

Note: People often seem to have difficulty distinguishing between the terms stepsister and half-sister, etc. If you are making a will to include your siblings the distinction is very important. A half-sister is one with whom you share a common biological parent; a stepsister is one who has two entirely different parents. From the biological parent's point of view your half-brothers and half-sisters will fall within the definition 'my children' but the stepbrothers and stepsisters won't. In an intestacy situation brothers and sister of the whole blood are preferred to brothers and sisters of the half-blood which is another reason that the intestacy rules can often operate unfairly.

Illegitimate children

At one time illegitimate children did not inherit under a gift 'to my children.' It is not proposed to go over the old rules in this book but to refer briefly to the two statutes which replaced the old rules.

For wills made between 1st January 1970 and 4th April 1988 the position is governed by The Family Law Reform Act 1969. As a result of that Act any reference, express or implied, to a child of any person must be construed as including a reference to any illegitimate child. Likewise, any reference to a person related in some manner to another person must be read as if he or another person through whom the relationship is deduced had been born legitimate. In both these circumstances a contrary intention may be expressed in the will. There are two points to note here. Firstly, that the Act refers to dispositions specifically. The result is that a gift to 'my children' would include illegitimate children but an appointment of 'my

children' as executors would not because the appointment
of executors is not a disposition.

Secondly, the Act specifically stated that construction of
the word 'heir' was unaffected.

The Family Law Reform Act 1987 replaced the provisions set out in the 1969 Act. The result is that in wills
made after 4th April 1988 any reference to a relationship
between two people is construed without any regard to
notions of legitimacy or otherwise. The Act also extended
the provisions to include the word 'heir'. Note that for
wills made after 1st January 1970 and before 4th April
1988 the 1969 Act still applies.

There are likely to be cases where the effect of the old
rules still applies due to the age of the will. The case of
Timothy Everard Upton v National Westminster Bank,
Richard Tichborne Everard Upton and Rosalie Jane Prior
(2004) is an example. A grandfather made his will in 1930
and left three-fifths of his estate to his son who in turn
purported to leave it in his will to his illegitimate son
whom he had adopted during infancy. The son died first.
The son's executors disputed the child's claim to his
father's share of his grandfather's estate on the grounds of
illegitimacy. The court held that the reference to 'a child' in
the grandfather's will was a reference to legitimate children. No contrary intention appeared in the will. The
provisions of the 1987 amendments were not retrospective.
The share of the grandfather's estate which his deceased
son would otherwise have inherited therefore passed to the
surviving son and not to the deceased son's child.

Note: This case turned on the issue of illegitimacy.
The reader may be puzzled as to why illegitimacy was an
issue if he had been legally adopted by his father.
Unfortunately, the Adoption Act 1976, which would
otherwise have enabled the grandson to inherit, was not
retrospective either and did not apply to documents
executed prior to 1976.

It has to be said that the potential existence of illegitimate children can be a nightmare for executors. If a

testator leaves a gift to his children, how can they be sure that there are no illegitimate offspring in existence? It is kinder to them to name your children. Instead of a gift 'to my children' write 'to my children Fred Mary and Jane'. They may then safely distribute to the named beneficiaries without worrying that the description 'my children' extends further than your relatives knew. (However, see the later chapter on leaving somebody out for another problem this doesn't solve.)

Adopted children
Adopted children are regarded as children of the adopting family for all succession purposes. In essence, an adopted child is treated as if he had been born into the marriage. At the moment of adoption he loses his right to inherit from his birth family. However, there are saving provisions for rights that have already arisen.

Issue and descendants
The words 'issue' and 'descendants' are often found in home-made wills. Their legal meaning goes beyond your children and includes, grandchildren, great grandchildren and so on. For the sake of clarity, these words are best avoided. If you wish to benefit your grandchildren, it is better to say so in a gift separate from the one to your children.

Other people's children
You may wish to leave something to a friend's children. Perhaps you are childless and wish to distribute your estate between the children of other family members. Obviously, you can refer to your nephews and nieces as just that. You may also have godchildren who may be described as such although it is best to add their names. ('My godson Geoffrey Brown.') Be careful if you are leaving gifts to the children of more than one family. This is an area where the layman's interpretation can differ from the established legal rules of construction. A gift to 'the children of A and

B' will be construed as giving a gift to A's children and to B not to B's children. If you wish to leave the gift to B's children as well as A's children, it is necessary to say 'to the children of A and the children of B'. A more elegant way of doing this is to say 'to Mary, Jane and Anne Bloggs, children of my friend Roberta Bloggs and Fred, Michael and Andrew Jones, children of my friend Susan Jones'.

Minor children

There is a difficulty with leaving money to minor children which is that they cannot give a valid receipt until they are 18. You must, therefore, choose between including a provision that your executors may give the money to the parents and leaving the money in trust until a certain age. In a home-made will, trusts are best avoided although you can write a simple gift to a minor child as 'I give £500 to my godson Fred Jones on attaining the age of 18 years.' Do not attempt to set up a complicated trust arrangement. It is a recipe for disaster. The worst example of a home-made will I have encountered was an attempt to set up a discretionary trust coupled with various legacies and a separate trust of a different part of the estate. The most obvious difficulty was that the discretionary trust had only one beneficiary but the other provisions were complicated and muddled to such an extent that the case proved very lucrative for the lawyers.

A further refinement is that unless you specify that the gift carries the intermediate income, Fred does not get any interest on the funds even if he is a baby when you die. In contrast, pecuniary legacies to your own children do carry the income as of right.

If you leave your residuary estate to minor children, then the trustees will have to invest the funds until the children reach the specified age. This will be 18 unless you state that they are to receive their money at a later age. The trustees will need to consider the investments carefully in order to comply with their responsibilities under the Trustee Act 2000. Usually a balance will need to be struck between providing for income and ensuring an element of capital growth. Residuary gifts do include income arising from investment of the capital.

If your estate is likely to be of a fair size you may be well advised to consider postponing to either 21 or 25 the age when your children receive the money. The Trustee Act 1925 empowers trustees to release funds for the 'maintenance education or advancement of the beneficiary' so money can be made available for such things as university fees or driving lessons.

Divorcees

A decree absolute dissolves a marriage so that the couple concerned are no longer husband and wife. Divorce is, therefore, one of those occasions where it is essential to make a fresh will. Should you omit to do so, any gift to or appointment of your former spouse as executor will not take effect. For deaths after 1st January 1996 the law says that the former spouse is deemed to have died at the time the marriage was dissolved. This is always subject to a contrary intention in the will so if you feel you would still wish your former spouse to have your estate following a divorce you must say so.

It has to be said that testators can be very slow indeed to change their wills even when the circumstances would seem compelling to an outsider. Professional wills frequently include a reference to 'the gift failing for any other reason'. This is to cover the situation where divorce or other events prevent a gift from being given to the intended recipient.

Second marriages

With the trend for more and more second or even third, fourth and fifth marriages to take place the testamentary provisions can become very complicated. It must be said here that sentiment should never blind you to the possibility of your spouse undergoing a change of heart once you are dead. What you agree in the early days of your marriage may seem outmoded ten years after your death. It is therefore important to give consideration to the protection of any children from your first marriage as well as your surviving spouse.

EXAMPLE

Steve has two children, Jane and Katherine, from his first marriage. Some years after his first wife's death he meets and marries Susan. She has two sons, Brian and James, from her previous marriage. Steve and Susan agree that they trust each other. In particular they know that when one of them dies the survivor will see that all the children are taken care of. They decide to make wills leaving everything to each other and then dividing the estate between all four children on the second death.

Steve dies some years later and Susan gets everything he owned. Five years later she decides she should make a new will because she has some grandchildren from Brian. She decides that she would like to leave everything to her own children and grandchildren considering 'the time that has elapsed since Steve died'. In other words, to use a common phrase, 'that was then, this is now'. Steve's children are excluded and will probably not find out until years later when Susan dies. They will have an uphill struggle to try and get anything from Susan's estate.

An alternative scenario would be that Susan remarries some years after Steve's death. Her will would be revoked as a matter of law. She might then make a new will in favour of her new husband or omit to make a will altogether. If she died intestate, Steve's children would have no claim on her estate under the intestacy rules. Depending on the amount she left, either her new husband would get everything or he would share it with her own children.

The most basic way of protecting the interests of everyone concerned where there is a second marriage is a life interest will. This means that the assets of the first to die are placed into a trust and the surviving spouse receives the income but does not own the underlying capital. It is possible to specify that the trustees may resort to capital if the income proves to be insufficient. On the death of the survivor, the assets then belong to the beneficiaries specified in the first will and not the survivor's.

EXAMPLE

Mike and Jean meet and marry in their fifties. They are both widowed with children and grandchildren when they meet. They agree that their respective children should benefit from what they each brought into the marriage. Their wills are written so that on Mike's death Jean obtains an income from a trust into which all his assets are placed. Mike's will states that when Jean dies his children are to receive his assets between them subject to a legacy of £500 to each of his grandchildren then living. Jean's will is written under a similar arrangement.

There are various other elements which can be added to this arrangement where inheritance tax is a consideration. For instance, the trust may be confined to the nil rate band for inheritance tax or the widow's interest may be terminated if she remarries.

This type of life interest arrangement requires professional drafting at all times as the trust must be carefully worded. It does, however, offer protection to both the surviving spouse and the children from both marriages and is well worth considering. Professional trustees are strongly recommended in such situations since having the widow or children as trustees may lead to allegations of bias or self-interest in making financial decisions. At best having beneficiaries as trustees is likely to create a conflict of interests that they may find it uncomfortable to deal with.

Bankrupts

One of your children may have the misfortune to go bankrupt. If so, you need to consider what to do with any gift previously intended for him or her. If you leave your will as it is, then the gift will pass to the trustee in bankruptcy and be used to clear the bankrupt's debts. If you feel your child has been irresponsible or you feel you wish to see his creditors repaid, this may suit you. If it doesn't, you need to consider making other arrangements. Some people feel that leaving everything to the other children knowing they will take care of him is best. There are numerous reasons, including tax reasons, why this may not work. Probably the best arrangement is to place the bankrupt's share into a trust where he never obtains an outright interest. Seek professional advice as soon as possible.

Similar considerations may well apply to potential beneficiaries who have drink or drug problems or are simply likely to squander their inheritance at the bookies or even the local shopping mall! Remember that a trust costs money to set up and administer so the amount of money you wish to leave is a factor to consider, as is the level of problem the beneficiary has. Perhaps you could live with your child spending £200 on a 'booze cruise' but what about £10,000? With a trust of this type it is entirely possible for the trustee to pay funds over to the beneficiary if he or she needs them and to pay out the entire fund if recovery from addiction is achieved.

Criminals

Following changes to the previous law a criminal may now be a beneficiary under a will and is entitled to his or her legacy in full. However, this does not apply where the criminal concerned is the killer of the deceased. The general rule is that a person found guilty of the murder or manslaughter of another who is not found to have been insane at the time of the killing cannot take any benefit under his will. The reasons for this are obvious. Public policy dictates that a murderer cannot benefit from his crime. With manslaughter, the rule applies regardless of whether any moral blame can be attributed to the killer. What if the killer is found to be mentally disturbed? Where the killer has been declared insane the rule does not apply because a verdict of 'not guilty by reason of insanity' amounts to an acquittal of the accused.

If the killer forfeits his inheritance it passes according to the terms of the will or, failing that, under the intestacy rules.

EXAMPLE
Bill has three children: John, Charles and Molly. Charles is found guilty of the murder of his father following a family row which unfortunately escalated out of control. Bill's will stated that he left his estate 'to such of my children as are living at my death and if more than one in equal shares.' Under the forfeiture rule Charles is not entitled to have his share so John and Molly take the entire estate between them.

A survivor of a suicide pact would in all probability be caught by this rule. For the purposes of applying the rule, no account is taken of the killer's moral guilt or the motive or intention behind the killing. The result is that so-called 'mercy killings' would result in forfeiture as well.

Originally this was a rule created by judges. Later the rule was given statutory recognition in the Forfeiture Act 1982. The Act applies to deaths on or after 13th October 1982 and in one respect modifies the original rule. Under this Act the court may in certain circumstances give relief from the consequences of the rule but only with regard to unlawful killings other than murder. Murder always results in forfeiture. The relief is granted at the discretion of the court and is not a foregone conclusion. As stated above, the forfeiture rule applies to manslaughter regardless of the moral guilt. From time to time, manslaughter charges can arise in circumstances where the opinion of the general public might be sympathetic to the defendant. It is for this reason that the court has the discretion to grant relief from the rule in some instances.

As with divorce you will frequently see professional wills including the phrase 'if my wife shall fail to survive me by twenty eight days or the gift to her shall fail for any other reason I give . . .' to cover this contingency.

One further point to note here is that, unlike the provisions for divorce, the rule does not operate as if the killer had died before the testator. In a fairly recent case the child of a killer was held not to be entitled to take the testator's estate in place of his father. If his father had died before the testator in the normal course of events he would have stepped into his father's shoes and inherited what was due to him. As the rule works by way of barring the killer from benefit and not by deeming him to die before the testator, the son was excluded from benefit. That particular case being an intestacy, the estate passed to the persons next entitled. One might comment that this is a clear example of the sins of the father etc., etc.

Animals

This is an area where feelings tend to run a little high. Those people who do not own or care for animals will never see eye to eye with those who worry about the fate of their animals on their own death. Further, a testator who leaves everything to his animals or to a cat sanctuary is generally the cause of much fuss in the media. The epitaph 'eccentric' is almost certain to creep in somewhere.

The general problem with leaving funds to an animal is that the animal cannot give a receipt to the executors. As a matter of trust law there is a problem because a trust must have a beneficiary capable of enforcing it. However, the animal lover need not despair because English law has provided an exception to the general rule and a trust for the maintenance of a particular animal for its lifetime is valid. The trust must be limited in time to a period of 21 years so as to avoid falling foul of the rule against perpetuities because an animal cannot be a life in being for the purposes of that rule. Those who wish to learn more about the technicalities of this point should consult one of the standard books on trust law. Otherwise it may simply be noted that 21 years from the testator's death should be a sufficient period for the average cat or dog to live out its days in comfort. The keeper of giant tortoises or elephants may need to seek legal assistance with the drafting of a suitable arrangement!

Remember that you will need somewhere for the money to go when the animal dies. Often this will be an animal charity but could be anyone. For instance, you could leave 90 per cent of your estate to your children with a trust of 10 per cent for your dog and a gift over to your children on his death (i.e. when the dog dies, your children inherit what remains of the trust). It is important to state that the trust is for the animal's natural life otherwise Tiddles may find himself making a premature visit to the vet's surgery. Euthanasia recommended by a vet to avoid suffering at the end of the animal's life would be permitted though since this may be deemed the end of natural life.

Charities

Charities and similar organisations may benefit from your will. It is important to specify the charity's details correctly as there are many organisations with similar names or areas of operation. Ideally you should specify the name, address and registered charity number. These details can be obtained from the charity's literature or from the Charity Commission's website. This is one of the areas where a few minutes spent checking the details can save hours of work, argument and expense after your death. Some of the national charities have separately registered branches and it is usually the rule that the funds are left to the head office with a specification that the funds are used for your local branch. Check the rules with your local branch so that you can be sure your wishes are achievable. A lot of charities produce literature with specimen clauses for wills.

Due to the way charity law in England works there are many worthy organisations that are not registered as charities. This may not always be apparent as their litera- ture, campaigns and activities will not necessarily be any

different from those of a registered charity. Frequently the
only difference is in the ability to lobby for actual changes
in the law. Examples of this include anti-vivisection
organisations, groups such as the League Against Cruel
Sports and groups campaigning for the rights of the
unborn child. Conversely, some groups with controversial
aims are registered charities as they have managed to
bring themselves within the necessary statutory defini-
tions. For the purposes of a will the big difference is that
only those organisations accepted as charities by the
Inland Revenue are exempt from inheritance tax. This
distinction is therefore only likely to bother you if you are
planning a charitable gift as part of tax planning.

You may if you wish leave your entire estate to your
executors to allocate between charities of their choosing.
This course of action is not recommended as your executors will quickly be inundated with literature and begging
letters from hundreds of charities who have been made
aware of the terms of the will. On this point I speak from
personal experience. Within days of publication of the will
both my office and the executors' homes were inundated
with brochures and letters from dozens of charities. Sifting
through them to establish some criteria for final selection
was a huge task. Fortunately both executors agreed as to
the criteria to adopt but what if they had had different
views as to what the testator would have agreed with?

It is wise to specify what is to happen to the money if
the chosen charity has ceased to exist or has changed its
name or merged with another. Clarity is again the order of
the day. It is a true but regrettable fact that charities can
act in a most uncharitable manner when large sums of
money are at stake. In this they are no different from any
other class of beneficiary.

Given that a gift to a registered charity is tax-exempt it
can be a last resort weapon in tax planning. If you have
done everything you can to avoid inheritance tax and there
is still a potential bill, leave the money to charity. Your
relatives will still miss out on the amount in question but

at least you are deciding where the money should go rather than leaving it to be paid into the general taxation pot.

If you are keen on benefiting charitable causes you may be interested in a couple of schemes operated by solicitors in conjunction with charities. The details are given in the Appendix.

Your employer

If your employer is an individual you may leave him a legacy in the usual way. If you work for a limited company it is possible to leave a legacy to the company. You may also leave a gift to your local authority. Such gifts may be for the purpose of carrying out their duties, e.g. a sum of money to maintain the roads or for the benefit of their residents. For instance, you may wish to leave a piece of land for use as a recreation ground or municipal garden. Be sure you are leaving a gift and not a problem. Is the piece of land suitable for the specified purpose and will it be capable of economic maintenance?

It is possible to leave money to the government but few would wish to do so. Indeed most people spend a considerable amount of time and money so that the government receives as little of their money as possible.

6

MAKING THE BENEFICIARIES JUMP THROUGH HOOPS

So you have decided who is to benefit from your generosity on your death and to what extent. What is the next thing to consider?

The most obvious thing is whether it is to be an outright gift or to be placed into trust. If making your own will the gift should be outright as setting up a trust should never be attempted without professional assistance. The only possible exception is to minor children where you may specify that the gift is to be made when they are 18. If you wish to extend this to a greater age it is best to seek professional help as the trust law implications then become more serious.

What, though, if you think that the beneficiaries should do something for you in return for their money? Alternatively, what if you feel you would like to leave something to someone 'if only his circumstances were different'. Perhaps you think the intended recipient drinks too much, follows the wrong path in life or is simply married to the wrong person? Can and should you impose limitations and conditions on the gift?

You may well take the view that since it is your money you should be able to say what happens to it and that this extends to controlling things from beyond the grave. Within limits, the law will go along with this. English law permits testators a lot of freedom of disposition but, as with many other areas of life, public policy sets the limits. A condition may also be simply incapable of being performed.

In law there are two different types of condition which may be imposed: one is a condition precedent, the other a condition subsequent. Which it is depends purely on the construction of the will. The broad difference is that if the condition must be complied with before the gift takes effect it is a condition precedent whereas if it is intended to bring an end to the gift on the happening of some event it is a condition subsequent.

The question of whether a condition is precedent or subsequent is important because of the effect it has on the gift in the will. A condition precedent which is void leads to a complete failure of the gift but a condition subsequent which is void means that the beneficiary takes the gift without needing to fulfil the condition and thus defeats the testator's intentions.

If the condition is impossible to fulfil it may fall to the court to decide whether the gift fails or not. The case of Watson v National Children's Home and others illustrates how this works. The testator, Mr Chambers, made his will in September 1974. He left one half of his estate to the National Children's Home. The other half of his estate was bequeathed to the National Canine Defence League on condition that his pets were looked after in the League's kennels for the rest of their natural lives. He attached a condition that if the League did not agree to take care of his pets the half of his estate he had left to them would go to the National Children's Home instead. At the time he made his will he had just one dog. By the time he died he had no pets as his dog had predeceased him. Court action followed to determine whether the League received the half share or whether the National Children's Home received the entire estate. The court held that as the condition was no longer capable of being performed it had become spent and the half share passed to the League.

A condition may also fail because the terms are uncertain, it is contrary to public policy or because it is what the law calls *in terrorem*, i.e. it is made as a threat to the recipient. On the other hand, a condition may be imposed for what the testator perceives as the beneficiary's own good. In one home-made will I dealt with a beneficiary who was known for her generosity to others was left a legacy of several thousand pounds on condition 'she spends it on a shopping trip in London'. The testatrix clearly thought that without this condition the recipient would simply give the money to others less fortunate. The beneficiary duly arrived in London and claimed her money before heading for the shops. How much was spent on herself and how much on gifts for others isn't known.

Uncertainty

Throughout this book it has been stated that the guiding principle in making a will must be certainty. There must be no room for doubt as to the will's meaning and intention. Some conditions which testators seek to impose may be couched in uncertain terms. It may be that it is difficult to ascertain in what circumstances a condition is to operate or if the events which are referred to have happened or not. As with most other aspects of wills the courts have considered the question many times and in relation to many types of condition.

The main types of condition which may lead to uncertainty are conditions as to residence, religion and behaviour. It is quite common for wills leaving a house to a beneficiary for life to contain a condition that the interest ceases on the beneficiary 'ceasing to reside there permanently'. Often the beneficiary is the widow of the testator or an unmarried adult child. Due to the difficulties arising from deciding when residence has ceased the professionally drawn will usually contains a provision that the trustees have the final decision as to whether the beneficiary has ceased to reside at the property.

Conditions which have been found to be sufficiently certain include a condition against becoming or marrying a Roman Catholic and conditions against marriage with specified persons. It may be taken from this that conditions against marrying a person of any other specified religion would also be certain. On the other hand, such conditions may well be deemed contrary to public policy in future as they surely breach modern thinking on discrimination. No doubt there will be a test case on that point before too long.

Conditions found to be uncertain over the years include a condition not to associate with certain specified members of the family, the beneficiary not to marry anyone not of the Jewish faith and renewing acquaintance with a specified person. At first glance it may seem inconsistent to say that a condition requiring someone not to marry a Roman Catholic may be certain whilst a condition not to marry a person of the Jewish faith is void for uncertainty. It would appear from the case law that the courts regard the expression 'Jewish faith' as itself too uncertain. This may seem surprising but consider the expression 'Protestant faith' and it may become less so.

Occasionally a testator may save a potentially uncertain condition by specifying that the opinion of an acknowledged expert may be deemed conclusive. In matters of religious faith this would be a person of suitable authority within that faith. For example, in the case of Re Tuck's Settlement Trusts, Public Trustee v Tuck the settlement document provided that if there was any doubt as to whether a person met the condition the opinion of the Chief Rabbi was to be sought.

In some instances the court may be prepared to hear evidence of how the testator practised his faith, the idea being that such evidence shows what he intended the beneficiary to do by way of religious observance. Further, in those faiths where there is a particular form of induction, such as baptism by immersion, it is possible for the court to say with certainty whether or not the required act has been performed.

As with many other aspects of wills the case law on conditions is continually evolving.

Public policy

There are some conditions which public policy requires to be ignored. A condition may be taken as being contrary to public policy if it is not in the interests of the state for it to be performed. This may, of course, vary from one century to another as public opinion on matters such as morality shifts.

I have dealt with a case in which the testatrix left her estate to her son 'on condition he divorces his wife'. Such a condition is contrary to pubic policy since public policy is to uphold the institution of marriage. This means that however much you dislike your in-laws you cannot make your legacy to your children dependent on the issue of divorce proceedings.

It would also be contrary to public policy to impose a condition separating a parent and child; a point confirmed by the House of Lords in Re Sandbrook when they held invalid a clause forfeiting the grandchildren's interest if they should 'live with or continue under the custody, guardianship or control of their father'. Perhaps you dislike your child's stepchildren. Unfortunately, you must resist the temptation to make your child's legacy conditional on the children being placed with an adoption agency.

Other conditions contrary to public policy include those which seek to prevent the donee carrying out public duties, including serving with the armed forces, and which incite the beneficiary to commit a crime or indulge in antisocial behaviour. There is also case law to the effect that an extravagant or wasteful condition may be pronounced contrary to public policy.

In terrorem

These are conditions which seek to coerce the beneficiary into complying with the testator's wishes. One example is a condition intended to prevent the beneficiary from contesting the will. A condition not to contest the testator's wishes is the sort of thing which appeals to the drafter of a home-made will. What better way to have the final word than to threaten to disinherit the family entirely if they try to go against your wishes? When such conditions go before the court it is necessary to consider whether the testator was merely trying to coerce the donee to go along with the conditions or whether he intended that his money should go elsewhere if the donee fails to comply.

In principle, a condition that a beneficiary who challenges the will loses any benefit under it is valid, certainly where there is a gift over on failure to adhere to the condition. (Cooke v Turner 1846.) A gift over simply means that the money is directed elsewhere in the event of the first gift failing. What though is the effect of a condition which would also result in the other beneficiaries losing their entitlement if one contested the will?

It falls to the drafter of a home-made codicil to give us an illustration of such a condition that set out to prevent a challenge to the will but was declared so uncertain that the court could not put an interpretation on it. Along the way it was also examined for repugnancy and opposition to public policy. The case in point is In the matter of Diana Margaret Gamon Nathan, deceased sub nom Andrew William Nathan v Sally Anne Leonard(1) Paul Leo Leonard(2) National Association for Mental Health(3).

A codicil is a document executed in the same way as a will and intended to make some changes to an earlier will without affecting its validity. For a number of reasons they are best avoided. In this case the deceased decided to add a home-made codicil to her will. The deceased owned half a house and the other half was owned by a couple called Mr and Mrs Leonard. In the body of the will she directed that the Leonards be allowed to live in the house for as long as they wished. After certain legacies, the residue of the estate was divided into three parts. The Leonards received two-thirds and the other third was divided between C and his children and three charities. For some reason, the testatrix decided to add a home-made codicil.

This directed that 'As a safeguard to my wishes and to protect them from any parties . . . should they wish to contest or disagree with my will' the entire residuary estate was to go to the Leonards absolutely if anyone contested or disagreed with the terms of the will. The last sentence of the codicil stated, 'This clause cannot be superseded and will only come into being if at any time during the life of the Trust or up to 80 years has elapsed.'

In the event C commenced proceedings under the Inheritance (Provision for Family and Dependants) Act 1975, claiming that he should receive additional provision from the estate. In return Mr and Mrs Leonard contended that the result was to pass the whole of the residuary estate to them subject to C's claim under the Act.

Three questions arose:

1. Did the paragraph beginning 'As a safeguard to my wishes' create a valid condition?
2. If so, had there been a breach of the condition?
3. If the answer to question 2 was 'Yes', was the gift over to the Leonards effective?

A quick reading of the above will shows that the result of C's decision to bring court proceedings would have been to disinherit not only C but the charities as well. Surprisingly, the court held that this did not in itself make the condition void for uncertainty. Further, although the existence of such a condition would obviously have a strong deterrent effect on a beneficiary wondering whether to bring an action that did not make the condition contrary to public policy. However, it was clear that some words had been left out of the final sentence and it appeared impossible for the courts to say what they might have been. As a result, the condition was void for uncertainty.

As the condition failed for uncertainty it was not necessary to determine the other issues but the judge went on briefly to express his views. He stated that C's action clearly breached the condition whether or not it was successful. Even assuming the court had the power to grant relief from forfeiture in favour of the charities it would not have considered it appropriate to do so given the clear wording of the codicil. It was apparent that the testatrix had intended all the beneficiaries to be disinherited if one of them contested the will in any way. The fact that C's claim had this result was no reason to deprive the gift over of its effect.

Common conditions
Leaving aside situations where you wish to try and separate your beneficiaries from their spouses or their faith, there are generally three main situations in which you may wish to impose conditions. These are:

1.   Where you are worried that your spouse will remarry after your death and disinherit your children.
2.   Where you wish a named person to take care of your pets or perform some similar service after your death.
3.   Where you wish to offer a beneficiary the chance to buy something from your estate (although, strictly speaking, this is an option not a condition).

Your spouse
It is perfectly acceptable to limit your widow's interest in the estate to her widowhood. You may also wish to specify that she loses her interest in the estate if she enters into permanent cohabitation with another man. However, determining exactly when such a situation has arisen may be trickier to decide. Your executors may find themselves with an awkward situation on their hands and some embarrassing questions to ask. Remember that if your wife's interest is to end on remarriage, the money must then go somewhere else. This raises the issue of a trust and anything other than the most basic arrangement will require professional drafting.

If you intend to leave your estate to your wife for life with a gift over to your children, you may well need professional executors; certainly you will need people who are not beneficiaries. This is to prevent conflicts of interest arising. As a general principle of trust law, trustees must maintain a balance between the interests of beneficiaries. Investing for income for the widow at the same time as preserving the capital against erosion by inflationary pressures requires a careful approach. There is no legal bar to a beneficiary being a trustee but it will often lead to arguments.

Your pets

This is a fairly common situation. Obviously you will wish to be certain that your pets will be well taken care of when you are no longer with them. You may feel that your friend gets on so well with your pet that you would like them to be together after your death. It may be tempting to leave your friend '£2,000 on condition he looks after my pets for the rest of their lives'. This is different from leaving money in trust for your pets as the money goes to your friend immediately on your death. This type of condition imposes an obligation on your executors to see that your friend complies. What will they do if he starts to take care of your animals, gets his cheque and then gives the animals to somebody else? It is generally better to say, 'I give £2,000 to my friend X and express the wish without imposing a binding trust that he will take care of my pets until the end of their days.' This imposes a moral obligation on your friend but not one which the executors are bound to monitor.

In contrast to leaving money for their upkeep, you may wish to have your pets put to sleep when you are dead. This needs to be stated in the will. In the absence of any specific statement of who is to do this, your executors will have to perform the task.

Options to purchase

You may feel that you want to give a relative the chance to buy your house or your car or other asset. It is usual to express this in the will by giving an option to purchase. This may be coupled with a direction that the buyer gets a reduction from the full market value.

Whether you offer a discount or not, you must obviously impose a time-limit on the person to whom the option is given. If you don't, your executors will not be able to proceed with the administration of your estate with any certainty as to what is to happen. It is usual to impose a period of something like three to six months from the date of your death.

EXAMPLES

'I direct that after my death my sister Freda Smith shall be given the option to purchase my house 52 Rose Walk at the market value as certified to my executors by a suitably qualified valuer who is familiar with property prices in the area. I direct that such option must be exercised within three months of my death by giving notice in writing to my executors.'

In the above example the decision must be notified to the executors within the specified period. This does not mean the purchase must be legally completed within that period. If you wish to have the deal completed within a set period you must say so.

'I direct that after my death my cousin Bert Smith shall be offered the chance to purchase my house 54 London Road at a price to be determined by a suitably qualified valuer familiar with property prices in the area. I direct that Bert must notify my executors within three months of my death if he wishes to purchase my house and that the purchase must be completed by the expiration of six months from the date of my death.'

'I direct that my nephew Patrick Smith be given the choice of six books from my library and that he notifies my executors of his choice within six months of my death.'

Should you wish to impose an unusual specific condition on a beneficiary it is best to take professional advice. What you have in mind may seem perfectly reasonable to you but the law may not regard it as so. On the other hand, a professional may be able to come up with a way of making the condition stick where you might have failed.

Really a home-made will should be very basic in its content. Keep it simple, resist the temptation to impose trusts and conditions or use fancy phrases.

7

LEAVING PEOPLE OUT

It is quite possible that you may wish to leave somebody out of your will. For instance, you may never have got on with your eldest son or you intensely dislike the man your daughter married and don't wish your money to go in his direction. There are implications in doing this and it requires careful thought.

English law actually grants the testator a lot of freedom of disposition. In countries where the civil law, rather than common law, forms the basis of the legal system, rules of forced heirship frequently apply. Briefly, this means that the law says that a certain portion of your estate must go to your spouse, another to your children and a small portion may be left as you wish. In England you may, if you choose, leave the entire estate to a close friend or to your dog. However, bear in mind that the disappointed beneficiaries will most likely seek to thwart your expressed intentions. There are two ways in which they may go about this. These are a direct challenge to the will itself and a claim to a share of the estate under The Inheritance (Provision for Family and Dependants) Act 1975.

Challenges to the will

Contrary to the impression frequently given in popular TV programmes and works of fiction it is actually quite difficult to challenge the validity of a will. Mere dislike of the contents is not enough. It is necessary to prove one of the following:

1.   The testator was not of sound mind.
2.   Lack of knowledge and approval of the contents of the will by the testator.
3.   Undue influence or fraud.

Unsound mind

In order for testamentary capacity (i.e. the ability to make a valid will) to be established, three things must exist at the same time. These are:

1.   The testator must understand and be aware of the nature and extent of the property he owns.
2.   The testator must understand that he is giving his property by will to one or more people or causes.
3.   The testator must also understand the nature and the extent of the claims upon him both in respect of people he is including in the will and those he seeks to exclude.

These conditions must exist both when he gives instructions for the will and when he signs it. Even so, if the testator's mental condition deteriorates between giving instructions and executing the will, it is sufficient to show that he understands he is executing the will in respect of which he previously gave instructions. It must be shown that the will has been drawn totally in accordance with the instructions and that the testator understands that he is signing a will made according to those instructions even if he can no longer follow every detail.

It is, of course, essential that the testator understand he is signing a will. To quote Cockburn CJ in Banks v Goodfellow (1870):

'It is essential to the exercise of such a power that a testator shall understand the nature of the act and its effects; shall understand the extent of the property of which he is disposing; shall be able to comprehend and appreciate the claims to which he ought to give effect; and with a view to the latter object, that no disorder of the mind shall poison his affections, pervert his sense of right, or prevent the exercise of his natural faculties – that no insane delusion shall influence his will in disposing of his property and bring about a disposal of it which, if the mind had been sound, would not have been made.'

So what if the disappointed beneficiaries wish to claim you were not of sound mind when you excluded them from your will? The Probate Registry will admit to probate any will which is rational on its face and executed correctly. No proof of capacity is requested unless the testator's capacity is challenged. The presumption is that the testator was sane. However, once sanity has been contested, the burden of proof shifts to the person seeking to propound the will, i.e. the person applying for the Grant of Probate.

EXAMPLE
John makes a will leaving everything to his son. His daughter Sarah lives overseas and as a result has seen him only rarely during the last few years of his life. She used to phone him fairly regularly and in the last few months of his life became concerned that he was becoming senile. On his death she is very upset to discover that he has left her nothing and is even more concerned to discover that the will was made just four months before he died. She consults her solicitor who asks her if her father was suffering from dementia at all. Once Sarah has raised the issue of mental capacity it is up to John's son to prove that his father had the capacity to make his will. This may involve a full-blown contested probate hearing or may be resolved pre trial by the production of a medical report. Whatever the outcome, a lot of bitterness and falling out between siblings may be caused.

In some instances, there may be a presumption against sanity. This is because English law presumes a state of affairs continues without interruption unless the contrary is proved. It follows that if you were known to be insane at a time prior to making your will, it will be presumed that you continued to be insane. The person seeking to prove the will must then prove that you had ceased to be insane when the will was signed. The presumption that you remained insane may be enhanced by the terms of the will itself. For instance, the dispositions may be such that no sane testator would dream of making them or they may be irrational. On the other hand, if the will makes sense and contains provisions that an ordinary person might well be expected to make, this can rebut the presumption of insanity. This being English law, a bit of eccentricity on the testator's part is permitted. It would appear from the case law that there is greater leeway granted to home-made wills in that regard.

For the purposes of making your own will it is probably not necessary to consider the issue of delusions since no testator acting in person is likely to consider he suffers from them. Suffice it to say that it is possible to make a will although suffering from a delusion unless the delusion is such as to affect the disposition of the estate. A person may have lucid intervals during which he can make a valid will but, again, the onus will be on the person propounding the will to prove it.

It is fair to say that as we grow older our mental faculties diminish and senility may affect the ability to make a will. The drugs used to treat illness may also have an effect on mental capacity. Strong painkillers, for example, may result in the would-be testator being 'not quite with it'. With an older person or somebody suffering from serious illness, it is essential to seek professional advice. Most solicitors preparing wills in those instances will seek to have either a report from a medical expert or ask the doctor to witness the will. This has been described by one judge as 'the golden but tactless rule'. In any event it is advisable for detailed notes of the testator's condition and the circumstances of execution of the will to be taken and kept with the will for future reference. The closer to death the testator is, the more important this becomes.

If you are contemplating making a will because you have recently been diagnosed with a terminal illness, you may consider it worthwhile to ask your doctor if he or she will be a witness to your signature. At least then the doctor may be approached for a statement by your executors in the event of a dispute.

Note that being an alcoholic or drug addict does not of itself mean testamentary capacity is lost but obviously such substances may cause mental impairment sufficient to lead to incapacity.

Lack of knowledge and approval of the will's contents

Little need be said about this ground for challenge since the person who writes his own will surely knows and approves of its contents. Generally, lack of knowledge will be pleaded where the testator was blind, deaf or dumb or not a native speaker of the language in which the will was written. Professionally drawn wills contain special attestation clauses to cover such situations. For example, the will of a blind testator will contain words to show that the will was read over to him before he signed it and that he signified his knowledge and approval of the contents. Where the testator does not speak English very well the will, although written in English, is read to him both in English and in his own language before he signs it. The attestation clause will state this. Where a testator makes his own will he will, of course, write it in the language he chooses. There is no objection to this but a certified translation will be required when the application for probate is made.

Another situation where this ground of challenge may arise is where the will is drawn up by a beneficiary who takes a substantial benefit under it. This is not to say that a person preparing a will for another can never benefit under it but that a suspicion arises which must be rebutted. In the case of Barry v Butlin (1838) it was stated that the will should not be upheld unless the suspicion was removed and the court satisfied that the document represented the true wishes of the deceased.

It may be that a testator making his own will cannot be said to lack knowledge of the contents but whether the contents represent what he intended may be open to doubt. In other words, the testator may think he has written one thing but the law reads it quite differently. Sometimes the meaning may be far from clear. If making your own will it is essential to avoid using legal terms you have seen or heard. You may think you know what they mean but you may be very wrong. Where the testator's intent is open to interpretation, the court may be asked to consider the meaning of the will in a construction summons. Although not requiring a construction summons the following is a real-life example of ambiguous wording from a home-made will: 'I give to the Salvation Army the clothes worn by my dear wife before she departed for paradise hanging in the wardrobe.'

Undue influence or fraud

This really comes down to the testator being pressurised into making a will in certain terms. It may be more readily inferred with an elderly or infirm testator which is the reason that a solicitor will insist on seeing your elderly parent alone.

Unlike sanity there is no presumption of undue influence. It is necessary to prove there was pressure sufficient to overwhelm the wishes of the testator. It is not enough to show that a relationship such as husband and wife, brother and sister or doctor and patient existed between the testator and the beneficiary. For one thing it is surely natural for a person to leave money to his spouse or child. If anyone wishes to allege undue influence he must prove it rather than the person propounding the will having to disprove it.

It is not uncommon for disappointed family members to try and allege undue influence. This is particularly so where an elderly person leaves his estate to a neighbour, for example, who has cared for him during his final years. The family member concerned may not have seen the deceased for many years but will often consider that something underhand has taken place. He may then try to allege undue influence but it is an unwise man who alleges undue influence without reasonable grounds to support it. Specific acts of the alleged influence must be cited. For example, if acts of violence are alleged, details of the incidents must be provided. It should also be noted that undue influence on the testator to leave money or goods to another party may be alleged. For example, a woman might exert pressure on the testator to leave money to her child.

It will be seen from the above that challenging a will is not that easy and will inevitably cause ill-feeling in the family. Moreover, the costs of litigation can soar as the arguments drag on. Aggrieved family members may therefore try to bring themselves within one of the classes specified in the Inheritance (Provision for Family and Dependants) Act 1975.

The list of persons eligible to make application is set out in section 1(1) of the Act as amended by the Law Reform (Succession) Act 1995. Those applying under the Act make application for financial provision from the estate of the deceased on the grounds that the will or intestacy did not make reasonable financial provision for them.

1. The wife or husband of the deceased.
2. The former wife or husband of the deceased who has not remarried.
3. A cohabitant of the deceased.
4. A child of the deceased.
5. Any person (not being a child of the deceased) who, in the case of any marriage to which the deceased was at any time a party, was treated by the deceased as a child of the family in relation to that marriage.

6.   Any person (not being a person included in the above) who immediately before the death of the deceased was being maintained, either wholly or partly, by the deceased.

The application of this Act and the numerous cases decided under it would make a book in itself. For the purposes of making your will, you need simply to be aware of the existence of this Act and the classes of people who can apply. You need also to consider carefully your reasons for leaving them out and whether they can be upheld. It is strongly recommended that if you wish to omit someone from your will you seek professional advice unless the reasons for doing so are overwhelmingly compelling.

Let us take a brief look at the categories set out above.

Spouse
You will obviously want to know that your spouse can survive financially after your death. You may have entered into a second marriage after the death of your previous spouse or you may have been divorced. In Chapter 5 we have considered provision for the survivor in these situations and the benefits of a life interest over an absolute gift. If your spouse is adequately provided for because she has substantial assets in her own name or you have generous death-in-service benefits that will go to her, omitting her from the will may not be unreasonable. There may often be tax reasons for leaving assets to your children rather than your surviving spouse. If your combined estates are over the inheritance tax threshold, then it makes sense to utilise the nil rate band for inheritance tax in each will by benefiting persons other than the surviving spouse.

Former spouse
A former spouse is defined as a former husband or wife whose marriage with the deceased was dissolved during the lifetime of the deceased either under the law of any

part of the British Isles or outside the British Isles by a divorce or annulment entitled to be recognised by the law of England and Wales.

Today most claims for ancillary relief in divorce proceedings would be settled on the basis that final orders of an income and capital nature would be made and the right to make a claim under this Act waived. If you are divorced, check your court order in the ancillary relief proceedings and see if it contains wording to this effect. If it does, then only in exceptional circumstances would an ex-spouse be able to claim.

Cohabitant

This section is limited in scope. The death must have occurred after 1st January 1996. The claimant must have lived in the same household as the deceased and as the husband or wife of the deceased. The cohabitation must have been for a period of two years immediately preceding the death of the deceased.

For the purposes of the two-year period it does not matter that the deceased may have spent some weeks in hospital prior to his death as long as the relationship was continuing. A separation of three months brought about by the circumstances of the deceased's illness was held not to render a claim inadmissible in the case of Gully v Dix (2004). In that case G lived with the deceased from 1974 until he died in October 2001. The deceased suffered from such a serious drinking problem that G effectively took care of him. In the August before his death the deceased threatened to kill himself with a knife and G was so frightened she went to stay with her daughter. After the deceased died G claimed provision from his estate. The judge found the 'settled situation' to be the 27 years of living together rather than the brief separation immediately prior to the death. The 1975 Act refers to living in the same household not the same house. As G was still bound to the responsibilities of the relationship she could be said to be living in the same household. There was evidence to the effect that both parties were still working on their relationship. The situation might have been very different had the parties involved regarded their relationship as having ended when they ceased living in the same house.

At present this category applies only to heterosexual relationships. It is possible this will change at some time in the future. Note that the absence of sexual activity is not necessarily fatal to a finding that the couple were living as husband and wife. In Re Watson (1999) the couple had lived together for many years but, as with many couples, had ceased sexual relations as they got older and actually slept in separate rooms. The court stated that account should be taken of 'the multifarious nature of marital relationships' including the deceased's assumption of responsibility for the applicant.

A child of the deceased

This category includes an illegitimate child, a child *en ventre sa mere* (a child whose mother is pregnant with him) at the date of death of the deceased and an adult child. A child may not claim if he is adopted between the date of his parent's death and the date of his application.

The child of a void marriage is also entitled to claim, provided that at the time of his conception his parents believed the marriage to be valid.

With a child born in wedlock, the husband of the woman is treated as the father unless the contrary is proved.

The Human Fertilisation and Embryology Act 1990 sets out various provisions which cover the situation where conception takes place by artificial means. The provisions are complicated but, as a general rule, where both parties to the marriage consent to the treatment the husband will be treated as the father of the child. In cases where paternity is disputed, it is possible to make application to the court for a declaration of parentage.

It is somewhat difficult to say with certainty whether adult children must be in financial need in order to succeed under this Act. The case law has not always been consistent on that point. A child who was very wealthy in his own right would probably not succeed in an application unless there were compelling reasons for him to receive provision and certainly not if there was a relatively modest estate with a widow relying on the money.

It should be noted that the law does not require you to treat all your children exactly the same. It often happens that one child in a family does better for himself than another. This may be due to obtaining higher grades at school or by starting a successful business. Sometimes it may come down to making a good marriage. In these circumstances it is not unreasonable for you to divide your estate unequally so that the better off child receives a smaller portion of the estate. For the purposes of saving inheritance tax, generation skipping is often advisable. Why leave funds to a comfortably placed child so as to increase his eventual estate for the taxman? It may be a better idea to leave a large part of your estate direct to your grandchildren or into a trust for them. In such circumstances a family discussion before the will is drawn up may avoid a lot of bad feeling on the death. Remember that, in the immediate aftermath of a death, people do not always think rationally. What may come to make perfect sense with time may initially cause them great distress.

Any person treated as a child of the family

This phrase is not defined in the Act. It has been taken as including an adult stepson (Re Callaghan). It also appears that the treatment of a stepchild by the surviving step-father or stepmother after the death of the natural parent may be a relevant factor in deciding whether the applicant qualifies as having been treated as a child of the family.

You may be surprised to learn what relationships the court can come up with. For example, in some cases a grandparent may be said to have treated the applicant as his or her own child. In Re A (a child of the family) the grandchild was allowed to claim provision from the grand-father's estate, it being held that the grandparents had assumed primary responsibility for the child. Over-indulgent grandparents beware!

In discussing the possibility of a claim from a member of this category we come back to the question of second marriages. The scenario it is vital to avoid is leaving everything to your second wife and relying on her to treat your children equally with her own. Couples often make mirror wills leaving everything to each other initially and then to the children on the second death. This is the very common scenario of 'everything to my wife provided that if she shall predecease me I give everything to such of my children as are then living and if more than one in equal shares'. Such an arrangement is fine until the surviving spouse meets somebody else or simply changes her mind and makes a new will.

Bear in mind that, on the one hand, you do not want your children to have to bring such an action against your widow's estate and, on the other, you may well wish to avoid an action against your estate by her children. Great caution is required if conflicting interests are to be balanced and satisfied.

Any other person
This is the category under which a secret mistress can make a claim. The applicant will need to satisfy the court that she was being maintained either in whole or in part by the deceased immediately before the death and also the extent to which the deceased had assumed that responsibility.

It is a question of fact whether one person made a substantial contribution to another person's needs. The applicant must satisfy the court not only that such mainte-nance is paid but that the deceased had assumed responsib-ility for the maintenance of the applicant. It is not necessary for the applicant to prove that the deceased intended to go on maintaining the applicant after his death.

If you make periodical payments to another for any reason it may be a sensible precaution to give written indication to him that he should not rely on such payments continuing for any length of time. For example, you may give money to a relative who has fallen on hard times and needs assistance paying his mortgage. Helping him out until he is back on his feet is kind of you but should perhaps be done on the basis of 'I'll help you out when and where I can but don't rely on it.'

What not to say
Having read the foregoing you may still feel you wish to omit somebody from your will and that you can justify this. We have seen that sometimes this can be acceptable. It is essential to bear in mind that a will becomes a public document once probate has been granted. Anybody can obtain a copy from the Probate Registry. This means that however deep your dislike of your relatives may run it is wiser not to spell this out graphically in your will. The Probate Registry will not admit to probate words which are deeply offensive or libellous in any event.

If you have what you consider to be sound reasons for omitting someone, it is better to place these in a letter to be stored with your will. Your reasons will then be made known without the general public getting to see them. If court action should follow your death, then such a letter is evidence of your reasons but is not binding on the court.

Examples

'In my will dated 1st of October [year] I have made no provision for my son Michael. This is because I have given him the sum of £50,000 during my lifetime to provide working capital for his business venture. Given that he has had such a generous gift in my lifetime and that he is doing well in his business as a result I feel that my other two children, who have received no such gifts, are entitled to split my estate between them.'

'In my will dated 5th November [year] I have left everything to my daughter Jane and nothing to my other daughter Sarah. As I have not seen or heard from Sarah for some ten years I feel that she no longer wishes to be a part of my life. To my mind it follows that she has no claim on my money or effects.'

You may also wish to include an assurance to your children that the lack of provision for them is not due to any lack of love or affection but for practical reasons concerning their financial positions relative to others with a claim on your generosity such as your widowed mother or your grandchildren.

Example

'In the will I have made today I have given everything to my grandchildren. I wish to assure my dear children that this is not due to any lack of love for them. I am aware that both of you are doing very well in life and have no need of additional funds at the moment. I feel that leaving my money in trust for my grandchildren will assist with their education and upbringing and by relieving you of a financial burden give you a benefit as well. I feel that this is better for everyone and my understanding is that it will save some tax as well.'

If you are leaving everything to the local animal sanctuary or to a major charity in preference to your family you will need to be certain that your reasons for overlooking your family are sound indeed. The fact that you prefer the company of your pet to that of your family is not likely to suffice. It is worth noting that gifts to registered charities are exempt from inheritance tax so that a gift to a charity may be useful if you have an inheritance tax liability.

Another way of approaching the question of provision for people you dislike is to leave them a token gift or a gift of something that will involve them in expense. For example, one irate testator left a stone each to the Collector of Taxes and to the Inspector of Taxes with the words 'now try getting blood out of that'.

If you leave a beneficiary a legacy of a specific object, then he is responsible for collecting it from your executors or having it delivered. If you are kindly disposed towards him, you will add the words 'free of tax and costs of delivery', leaving your estate to foot the bill. If, on the other hand, you are trying to avenge some wrong suffered in your lifetime you may care to leave some testamentary white elephant to be collected at the beneficiary's expense. Grand pianos are a particularly good way of achieving this due to their size and the cost of transporting them but the author once saw a pair of hideous china pug dogs used to good effect!

If all else fails, you could follow the example of the man who wrote in his will, 'To my ex-wife whom I promised to mention in my will "Hello".'

In conclusion, it is important to lay to rest what seems to be a popular myth which is the idea that leaving someone a token amount prevents him bringing a claim under the 1975 legislation. It doesn't because it is open to him to claim he has not been adequately provided for by the token gift. On the other hand, a token gift coupled with a letter setting out your reasons may well involve him in an uphill struggle to do so and is thus worthy of consideration. The important thing is to be subtle. Writing, 'I leave nothing to my eldest daughter because I cannot stand that bearded twerp she insisted on marrying and do not wish him to benefit from my money,' is likely to cause your executors great trouble. Writing, 'Despite my initial reservations about her marriage my daughter appears to be more than adequately provided for and I am therefore leaving her just my collection of unusual cork-screws in the hope she will treasure them as much as I have', may well serve you better. There are, of course, no guarantees. The post-death behaviour of the deceased's relatives is legendary amongst probate lawyers and a judge can always have a bad day.

8

OTHER MATTERS TO CONSIDER

There are a number of other matters you may wish to include in your will.

Testamentary guardians

If you have children under the age of 18 it is important to consider their welfare should an unfortunate accident leave them alone. This may not be something you wish to contemplate but, as with other aspects of making a will, a clear statement of your wishes can avoid much argument and heartache should the worst happen.

As and from 14th October 1991 such appointments are governed by the Children Act 1989. Under section 5 of that Act a person with parental responsibility for a child may appoint a guardian for that child in the event of his death. The term 'parental responsibility' means all the rights, duties, powers, responsibilities and authority which by law a parent of a child has in relation to the child and his property.

There is a difference for this purpose between a legitimate and an illegitimate child. Both parents have equal responsibility for a legitimate child, whereas the parental responsibility for an illegitimate child rests with the mother. The father of an illegitimate child may attain parental responsibility by a court order or by the drawing up of a parental responsibility agreement between him and the mother. Subsequent marriage will also confer responsibility.

Where a child has two parents with responsibility for him, the appointment of a guardian by will cannot override the rights of the other parent. The appointment will not take effect until the death of the second parent. The only exception to this is where the parent who dies had a residence order in his favour in force immediately prior to death. Residence orders are imposed during proceedings under section 8 of the Children Act to settle arrangements as to where a child shall live.

It is important to note that an appointment of guardians, by will or otherwise, must be dated. We have seen that forgetting to date the will is not fatal to its validity but that it is always a good idea to do so. Given the obvious wisdom of dating the will it may be thought that a problem is unlikely to occur in relation to appointment of guardians. However, it has also been explained that a mistake on the testator's part as to the date does not render the will invalid although it may lead to other problems. It is thus possible to envisage circumstances in which the will itself may be valid but the appointment of guardians is invalid due to the will bearing a date somewhat different from that on which it was actually executed.

A word may be added here as to whether it is advisable to have the same people appointed as guardians and executors/trustees. There is no legal bar to such a course of action but it may not necessarily be the best course of action. In my view it can often lead to a conflict of interest. The children may be very young when orphaned and the guardians face years of looking after them. Under the Trustee Act 1925 funds may be made available for the 'maintenance education or advancement' of the children during their minority. At the same time, the trustees have a duty to invest the funds wisely so as to maintain their value. It is not uncommon for beneficiaries to query the trustees' investment policy when they come of age. Where investments are concerned hindsight is, of course, a wonderful tool but nevertheless the burden on trustees is enormous. If they simultaneously have to cope with the financial cost of raising the child as one of their own, a conflict of interests may arise and mistakes of judgment may occur.

It is probably an excellent compromise to have one professional trustee and one family member trustee who may or may not be the guardian. This means that you have an expert on the intricacies of trustee law and investment to offer guidance and a trustee who is familiar with the family circumstances on a day-to-day basis.

Guardians must not use the child's funds to benefit themselves so it is important to consider whether you wish to make a gift to the guardians in their own right. Funds released under the Trustee Act for the maintenance, education and advancement of the children may be used only for those purposes. This will generally cover day-to-day living expenses, school fees and such matters as holidays and school trips. What though if the guardians need a bigger house? Although the law does not say that the children must reside with their guardian this is what would almost certainly happen in practice. The guardians may well have children of their own. They may suddenly be faced with an extra two or three children to care for with a resultant lack of space. For this reason you should consider whether to make an outright gift to the guardian, either by a pecuniary legacy or a share of your residuary estate. Alternatively, you may provide for your trustees to make loans to your guardians for the purpose of extending the house or buying another, larger residence. It goes without saying that in that situation the guardians and trustees must be different people.

Another way of coping with this potential problem is to enhance the trustees' administrative powers so as to enable them to invest some of the children's money in the purchase of a house to be used as a residence for them.

What you should never do is leave your entire estate to the appointed guardians and leave them to account to the children at a later date! Apart from any other considerations this is a bad idea for tax reasons.

If you wish to do anything other than leave a straight-forward legacy to the guardians it is best to seek professional advice. In contrast to executors there is no presumption that a gift to testamentary guardians depends on their being required to take up their duties.

Organ donation

You may wish to donate your organs for transplant purposes or you may be opposed to such an idea. It is not unusual for testators to request a solicitor to include such a provision in their will. The practical difficulty is that your will may not be immediately to hand when the question of donation arises. An expression of wishes in your will is therefore of value only if you have also told your nearest relatives what you have done. An organ donation card is of much greater value.

Medical research

Some people feel that they would like to be of service to medical science by donating their bodies for teaching or research purposes. If this is your wish, you must make contact with your nearest medical teaching hospital as there are specific formalities to comply with. A particular set of forms has to be completed and a copy filed with your will. On your death your relatives must notify the teaching hospital immediately so that arrangements for collection of the body can be made.

If you choose to go this route, you will not be able to have a funeral in the conventional sense although your relatives will almost certainly arrange a memorial service. The university concerned will arrange burial or cremation of the body once it has been finished with.

Graves

If you wish to be buried, it may worry you to think of your grave being neglected in the future. There is not a great deal you can do about this problem because of English law's insistence that things must happen within a maximum period of time. This rule is known as the rule against perpetuities and is not something that needs be examined in any great detail here. A gift which is charitable is not subject to the same limitations. It follows that if you can set up a gift for the maintenance of the fabric of the church in such a way as to include your grave or tomb, you are home and dry.

You can leave your executors a fund from which to pay for the upkeep of your grave for a period of 21 years. Remember that any remaining funds will have to go somewhere at the end of those 21 years. Alternatively, you could leave a gift to a beneficiary on condition that he maintains your grave, with a gift over to somebody else if he fails to do so. This has been held to be effective where the gift was given to one charity with a gift over to another charity. It will, of course, impose a burden on your executors as they will need to monitor compliance.

Perhaps the best way is to leave your executors a sum of money with a direction to enter into a maintenance agreement with a local authority. This is possible under The Parish Councils and Burial Authorities (Miscellaneous Provisions) Act 1970 whereby a local authority or a burial authority can enter into such an agreement on payment of a sum of money. Although the local authorities are not obliged to enter into such agreements, it is a way of having your grave maintained for 100 years in areas where they operate.

Administrative arrangements
In any professionally drawn will there will be a number of administrative clauses. The purpose of these is to enable the executors/trustees to deal with the administration of your estate efficiently. In some instances the statutory powers under the Trustee Act 1925 as amended by subsequent legislation are inadequate and need to be extended or modified. Conversely, some case law has imposed requirements that it is felt necessary specifically to exclude.

In days gone by, it was not unusual for such clauses to take up several pages of the will as the draftsman attempted to cover every possible scenario that might arise. The general feeling seemed to be that what you left out might be of more serious consequence than what you put in. James Kessler QC then produced a standard set of administrative clauses for the Society of Trust and Estate Practitioners which could be incorporated by reference. A lot of professionals have adopted these, with the result that modern wills are often shorter than they would otherwise have been.

You will probably not need to worry too much about administrative provisions when making a home-made will. Generally speaking, you will not need them if all the gifts in your will are to be given outright on your death since they are of most relevance to ongoing trust situations. It is probably better, on balance, to rely on the provisions contained in statute law than to attempt to dabble with inserting special powers for your executors.

9

POST-EXECUTION
CONSIDERATIONS

So you have chosen your words carefully, written your will in your best handwriting, chosen your witnesses for their good health and ability to give a coherent version of events and signed and dated your will. What next?

It goes without saying that there is no point in making a will if nobody knows you have done so. It is quite common for clients to tell their solicitors that they don't wish their spouse or their children to know they have made a will. This may in part stem from the fact that even today, when all sorts of taboos have been broken, death is still a subject that a lot of people prefer not to discuss. I was recently told by a funeral director acquaintance that he had received a complaint from a mother that her young daughter had looked down from the top of a bus and seen a coffin being carried into his premises. Contrast this with the seemingly acceptable images of sex and violence thrown at young people daily and the strength of this taboo becomes clear. It seems pointless to make a will and then not disclose the fact. Imagine how you would feel if, after going to all the trouble of making a valid will, your estate was administered in intestacy.

If you do wish to keep the existence of the will secret during your lifetime at least make sure it can be found after your death. It should be clearly marked as your will and stored in a prominent place. Perhaps you have a file where you keep your personal papers such as your passport and building society passbooks or you are in the habit of stuffing things in your bureau drawer. Think where your family would be likely to look for important papers after your death. Remember that your death may not come at a time or place where you expect it. You may not have the opportunity to put your affairs in order as so often quoted in the movies.

It is very helpful to your executors if you draw up a list of your assets and liabilities to place with the will. There is a simple assets log on page 129. You should update this from time to time as your investments change. The whereabouts of your title deeds should be included in the list although paper deeds are gradually being phased out following the introduction of electronic storage by the Land Registry.

You may also wish to keep with the will a list of people to be notified of your death so as to be given the opportunity of attending your funeral. Some years ago I was dismayed to have a letter to a friend returned by a solicitor with a letter to say that the friend had died. The lady concerned had always spent several months of the year travelling the world and so was often out of touch for weeks at a time. It seemed nobody had located her address book to contact those who might want to attend her funeral. Several people were thus denied the opportunity to pay their last respects to someone they had known for over 20 years.

A word of caution: if you do keep a list of assets or people to invite to your funeral, do not attach it to your will. When the will goes to the Probate Registry any marks which may indicate that something else has been attached to it at some time may cause problems. The suspicion is that there may have been a codicil attached. For this reason do not attach anything to your will by means of a paper-clip, pin or staple.

The executors need not know the contents of your will until after your death. Indeed, it is probably wise never to mention the contents of the will to anyone. Married couples will generally discuss the contents of their wills, of course, in order to decide the ultimate destination of their property. Otherwise, keep quiet. Never give anyone the opportunity of challenging your will at a later date; there have been numerous instances of people going to court over promises made to them that did not get fulfilled in the will. All they need to know is that you have made a will and that you have stored it in a certain place. It may be a good idea to provide your executors and/or family with a copy of the will in a sealed envelope so that they can refer to it immediately after your death. They may, for example, want to check the will for funeral wishes at a time when the original is not readily available. If you have made and stored your will at a solicitor's office and your death occurs at a weekend it is unlikely the original will be accessible immediately. Likewise, if the only copy is at your house there may be circumstances in which the executors cannot obtain ready access to it.

This assumes that you have told your executors of their appointment. Although not essential it is highly advisable to warn them of their appointment and, indeed, seek their consent to act before naming them in your will.

Changing your mind

Suppose you make a will and later decide you want to do something different? Perhaps your circumstances have changed? Forget about making a codicil; the best thing is to start again with a completely fresh will. For one thing, making a codicil cutting down the entitlement of a beneficiary is asking for trouble. Remember that on your death the will becomes a public document. If a beneficiary can see that he was originally left a bigger share of your estate, this gives him the opportunity to claim that a later codicil was executed under undue influence or with lack of capacity.

There are a number of ways in which a will can be revoked. Firstly, if you make a new will the previous will is revoked by operation of law. Professionally drawn wills always include a revocation clause. If you have separate

wills for English assets and foreign assets, care is needed to
ensure that only the correct will is revoked.

Secondly, a will may be revoked by declaring in writing
an intention to revoke an earlier will. This must be
executed in accordance with the Wills Act.

The third way of revoking a will is by the burning,
tearing or other destruction of a will either by the testator
or by someone at his direction and in his presence with the
intention of revoking it.

A will is also revoked by subsequent marriage unless it
has been drawn up and executed in contemplation of the
marriage and contains a statement to that effect. Divorce
revokes an appointment of the divorced spouse as executor and also cancels a gift to him. In any event, marriage
and divorce are two of the occasions on which you must
take a fresh look at your will. Other occasions include the
birth of a child and if you inherit or win large sums of
money.

By far the best way of dealing with revocation of a will
is by making a fresh one. You can make as many wills as
you wish during your lifetime but it is essential that it is
possible clearly to identify which is the last one. Most
solicitors will retain photocopies of your earlier wills with
your current one for evidential purposes. If, for example,
the last will is challenged, copies of the earlier ones may
show a clear pattern of testamentary gifts. This may go a
long way to refuting allegations of undue influence or lack
of testamentary capacity. When making your own will it is
important that the last will is easily identifiable. It is
probably better to destroy all previous wills to avoid any
confusion. If you are worried about any possibility of a
challenge you could make copies of earlier wills and write
'revoked' across the top.

10

WHEN PROFESSIONAL HELP IS ESSENTIAL

There are a number of situations in which it is absolutely vital to seek professional assistance either because the result you want to achieve is too complicated for home-drafting or your assets are of a type to which special tax concessions apply. The following sections should enable you to identify these situations and organise your paperwork before visiting a solicitor.

There are some common situations in which you will need more than a simple will:

1.   Where your estate is going to be over the threshold for inheritance tax.
2.   Where you have business assets.
3.   Where you have foreign assets.
4.   Where you wish to make provision for a handicapped child or a child with a problem such as a gambling addiction.
5.   Where you have a second family.

Tax
At one time only the upper classes paid death duties. The ordinary man in the street never had to worry his head about such matters. Unfortunately, the rise in home ownership coupled with the increase in house prices has led to a large increase in the number of estates paying tax. The Chancellor of the Exchequer fixes a starting point for inheritance tax in his annual budget. The amount below

that starting point is referred to as your 'nil rate band'. If your estate goes over that limit you will pay tax on the excess. The important thing to remember is that inheritance tax is by and large a voluntary tax; it is perfectly acceptable to write your will in such a way that the tax is reduced or eliminated.

The most basic form of tax planning for husband and wife is to set up discretionary trusts of your nil rate bands in each will. This ensures that you both take advantage of your nil rate bands.

Anything passing from one spouse to another is currently exempt from inheritance tax but passing everything to your spouse can lead to the accumulation of wealth in the survivor's estate. The resulting tax bill can be very big indeed. Where nil rate band trusts are set up the saving in tax can be substantial.

Example
Jim and Mary have assets worth £600,000 in total. Jim owns £350,000 of this and Mary owns the balance. If Jim leaves everything to Mary there will be no tax on his death as the spouse exemption will apply. When Mary dies, there will be a tax bill to pay and this will be on their combined estates minus her nil rate band. Jim's nil rate band has been wasted by passing everything to Mary.

In contrast, if the wills are written so as to utilise the nil rate band in each will, the tax bill will be much lower. On Jim's death the amount of his nil rate band will pass into the trust and the balance pass to Mary tax free. On Mary's death she will have her nil rate band set against her estate and only the balance will suffer tax.

There are various refinements that can be built into the trust. For instance, the house is frequently the main asset and it is possible to arrange matters so that half the house is placed into the trust. However, due to potential problems with the Inland Revenue it is important to have professional advice so that the trust does not fall foul of the anti-avoidance provisions. In particular, the Capital

Taxes Office has indicated that where there is half a house involved in the trust it will consider that the surviving spouse residing there has what is termed an 'interest in possession'. The effect of this is to negate the tax-saving advantages of this type of trust unless further steps are taken. At the time of writing, the problems can be resolved by setting up a debt or charge arrangement. In simple terms, this means that the trustees of the trust give the half share of the house back to the surviving spouse against a charge over the house, thus creating a debt between the two estates. The basic idea is simple but the paperwork required to execute it is complicated and needs careful drafting.

If nil rate band discretionary trusts are put into place, it is also necessary to convert a joint tenancy in the house into a tenancy in common. Should you enter into such an arrangement and then move house it is essential to purchase the new residence on a tenancy in common basis.

For couples with more valuable estates, further tax-planning measures will be required and may involve the use of lifetime trusts or gift and loan schemes. Where there are funds over and above that required for daily living, use may also be made of the potentially exempt transfer regime. In simple terms, that involves giving away sums of money and surviving the gift by seven years so that is not taken into account on your death.

Where tax is concerned, it should always be borne in mind that the security of the surviving spouse is more important than saving the tax bill on the second death. Nobody likes giving large sums of money to the taxman but there is no point in avoiding tax if your widow is forced to live in poverty as a result.

Business assets

If you own your own business there may be tax exemptions applicable so as to reduce the tax to nil on the business assets. Coupled with the availability of the nil rate band these can reduce your potential tax liability considerably but to take advantage of this a will requires careful drafting. If your business operates as a private company, you may wish to provide for an option to purchase to be written into the will. Alternatively, you may wish your executors to sell your business during the administration of your estate. The will needs to contain additional clauses to enable your executors to continue your business if you wish it to be sold as a going concern.

A properly drawn up partnership agreement will usually contain provision for what is to happen on the death of a partner. You cannot appoint a successor partner in your will.

Agricultural property also attracts a special exemption for inheritance tax but the rules are complicated. As with many other aspects of wills, the layman's idea of agricultural property does not necessarily coincide with that of the taxman.

Children with disabilities

There are some situations in which it is not possible to leave a beneficiary large sums of money in his own right. This may be due to the beneficiary's fondness for gambling, drug addiction or some form of mental incapacity. In other circumstances, it may be due to the perceived influence of another person in his life.

A major difficulty in leaving money to someone who lacks the mental capacity to handle his affairs is the fact he cannot give a valid receipt and discharge to the executors. The interaction with state benefits may also be a consideration.

There are a number of solutions and the route chosen may depend on several factors. For instance, if the intended beneficiary is already the subject of a receiving order under the Court of Protection, the Court will give directions as to the investment of the legacy. In that event, no special considerations arise for the will-drafter other than what amount it is wise to give.

If the intended legacy is only small, it may be acceptable to give it to another person in the will and entrust that person to use the money for the beneficiary's benefit. This may be done by a secret trust or a half-secret trust. A secret trust is one where the legacy is left to a named person absolutely but he has agreed with the testator that he takes the money for another person. Alternatively, the will may state that the named beneficiary takes the legacy 'upon the trusts' or 'for the purposes' that have been made known to him. In that event, the gift is on a half-secret trust as the trust is referred to but not explicitly revealed.

On some occasions, a parent may leave money to the other children in the family simply on the basis that he trusts them to take care of their brother or sister. In other words, an absolute gift with no notion of a trust other than reliance on their compassion for their sibling. Such an arrangement is fraught with potential difficulty and is best avoided.

Example
Fred and Mary have two children, Charles and George. Due to a head injury sustained during a childhood misadventure, George suffers from a certain degree of learning difficulties and cannot really be given half his parents' estate to deal with. Fred and Mary, therefore, decide to leave everything to Charles as they know he can be trusted to look after his brother. Initially everything goes smoothly and Charles gives George money when he needs it and makes sure he is taken care of. Unfortunately, Charles is later made redundant from his job. His industry is in decline and new job opportunities are few and far between, with fierce competition for any advertised vacancy. Charles struggles with his own finances and rising debts. Eventually, he is forced into bankruptcy and what funds he has left go to his creditors. As a result, George is also left in severe difficulties.

The problem in that example would have been avoided had a trust been set up for George in his parents' wills.

Other potential difficulties include a falling out between the children and the possibility of the able-bodied child dying before the other one without making adequate provision for him.

There are various types of trust arrangements that can be set up in this sort of situation and it is well worth talking them through with a professional. There is a category of trust known as a disabled trust, which attracts certain tax advantages, and this may suit your circumstances. Otherwise, the first choice to make is whether you wish to create a lifetime trust (an *inter vivos* trust) or to create a trust in your will (a will trust).

If you set up a trust during your lifetime, it need contain only a nominal amount of money. You then leave the trust an amount of money in your will. Mencap have a scheme whereby you pay for the setting up of a trust of which they are trustees. On death the money you wish to leave your child is paid into that trust and administered by them. The disadvantage of setting up an *inter vivos* trust is that it must be registered with the Inland Revenue's trust division immediately so that some time and possible expense is taken up each year dealing with a tax return.

With a will trust, the terms of the trust are contained within the will itself. The choice then becomes whether to make it an interest in possession trust or a discretionary trust. The essential difference is that with an interest in possession trust the beneficiary has 'the immediate right to the immediate income' (IRC v Pearson). In contrast, with a discretionary trust there is a class of beneficiaries who have no immediate entitlement to anything. The trustees then allocate funds as and when they see fit. It is usual to issue some kind of guidance to the trustees by way of letter or memorandum with the will but this must in no way fetter their discretion or the Inland Revenue will try and argue that the trust is really an interest in possession type.

If the problem is gambling or drug addiction rather than a mental or physical illness, a simple protective trust may fit the bill. This means that the money will be held by the trustees on terms that leave them to decide if, when and how the beneficiary receives his money.

Really it is impossible to say which type of trust is the best option. So much depends on the individual circumstances and the wishes and expectations of the testator. In some situations, the possible availability of state benefits will need to be considered. The tax implications of each route must also be taken into account. A full discussion with a trusts professional is essential.

Much the same considerations will apply in situations where you have responsibility for elderly or infirm parents and wish to make certain of their security if you should predecease them.

The second family

We have already touched on the problems that may arise from second marriages. There is always a balance to be struck between the security of the surviving spouse and the interests of the children from the first marriage.

The best way of protecting the interests of the children is to give the second spouse a life interest in the estate and provide for the capital to revert to the children on the second death. If both parties to the marriage write their wills this way, the interests of their own children will be protected. Of course, difficulties may arise if the estates of the spouses are of widely varying sizes so that one party to the marriage is more vulnerable to running out of funds. It is possible to allow recourse to capital but that requires sound investment decisions on the part of the trustees so as to avoid conflict between the surviving spouse and the children.

The alternative is to use the discretionary trust mechanism to set up a trust whereby the surviving spouse and children are all beneficiaries and the trustees can allocate funds between them according to the circumstances. Such a trust may continue throughout the life of the surviving spouse or may be terminated earlier. Where the estate is over the inheritance tax threshold, there is a charge to inheritance tax on every tenth anniversary of the trust coming into being. It is possible to reduce the impact of this charge by judicious timing of distributions and sound management of the investments.

Mirror wills and mutual wills

A lot of married couples appear to be under the impression that they require one will between them. The reality is that husband and wife must each sign a separate will. In most instances they will sign mirror wills, i.e. wills in identical terms. The most basic form of this is the typical scenario of: 'I give everything to my wife but if she has died before me I give everything to my children.'

Wills which are made in mirror form are not binding on the survivor who may change his or her will at any time. In second marriage scenarios many people draw up wills providing that if they have survived their spouse their estate is to be divided between their children and their spouse's children. The problem then is that there is nothing to stop them changing their will when their spouse is dead so as to remove their spouse's children from the equation.

Mutual wills are a different class of will from mirror wills. They may well be written in identical terms but, unlike mirror wills, they are intended to be binding on both parties. The law's requirement for mutual wills to be binding is very strict: there must be clear evidence of intention. Professionally drawn mutual wills contain a statement to the effect that they are intended to be irrevocable following the first death. Up until one of them dies the couple may change their wills as often as they wish. As soon as one dies, a trust arises which binds the survivor to comply with the terms. In reality, the survivor cannot be stopped from drawing up a new will if he or she wishes but will be bound by the terms of the trust; gifts incompatible with the original trust cannot be made so as to deprive the original beneficiaries of their inheritance.

The biggest drawback with mutual wills is their inflexibility. Circumstances may change between the two deaths so as to render changes in testamentary dispositions desirable. Tax rules may change and necessitate a reworking of the original scheme. If you are worried about protecting your children from the possible actions of your second spouse, a life interest trust in your will is a far better way than relying on the drawing up of mutual wills.

11

THE ADMINISTRATION OF YOUR ESTATE

Following your death there are various formalities to be dealt with. The following is just a brief overview as the main emphasis of this book is the preparation of a will.

On your death you will be certified dead by a qualified medical practitioner. He will give the medical certificate of death to your relatives. The next step is registration of the death, the person doing this being known as 'the informant'. There is an order of priority for this purpose. The nearest relatives have the first responsibility, with the person, if any, who was present at the death being first on the list. After that, the classes of informant include the person arranging the funeral and the proprietor of the premises in which the death occurred. It is common for solicitors to arrange funerals for deceased clients who have nobody else to do it for them. He or she will, therefore, register the death.

The Registrar of Deaths will hand the informant two pieces of paper. There is a white form for sending to the social security office for claiming outstanding state pension, etc. The other one is the green form required by the undertaker before the body can be disposed of. With cremation, two doctors are required to certify the fact of death before the funeral can take place.

Where the death has to be notified to the coroner, the procedure is different. This happens with a sudden, unexpected death or where foul play is suspected. A post mortem will be carried out and an inquest may be arranged. If there is to be an inquest, the coroner may issue an interim certificate of death to enable the funeral to take place and the probate process to commence. Only after the inquest, is the full certificate issued by the Registrar. The coroner's officer will keep the family informed as to the progress of the case and when the body may be released for burial or cremation.

An inquest will not always follow the involvement of the coroner. A post mortem may establish a natural cause of death so that the death certificate will be issued bearing the words 'after post mortem without inquest'.

Probate
Probate is the process by which your will is pronounced valid and your executors administer your estate. Where there is no will, the procedure is much the same except that the Court will issue a 'Grant of Letters of Administration' instead of a 'Grant of Probate' and you have no say in who obtains the grant. For intestate estates, the question of who is entitled to the grant is governed by the intestate succession rules. For example, if your spouse is alive he or she will be the person entitled. If you leave no spouse but several children, any one of the children may take out the grant. Where there is a minority or life interest involved, there must be two administrators.

If you are divorced with minor children, you need to be aware that failing to make a will could leave your former spouse in charge of your money on your death. This is because a person under 18 cannot take out a grant to your estate. There will need to be two administrators appointed to take a grant out on the child's behalf and the surviving parent will be the person with the prior entitlement. He or she will need to appoint a co-administrator. The grant will be limited until the child's 18th birthday when he or she will be entitled to take out a fresh grant if it is required for any reason.

Executors of a will take their authority from the will, and probate is confirmation of that authority. They are able to take up their duties from the moment of death. Where the estate is very small, they may be able to close bank accounts without formally obtaining a grant. In contrast, administrators take their authority from the Grant of Letters of Administration.

The first step is to notify all the interested parties that the death has occurred. Banks and building societies, company registrars and so on should be written to with the death certificate and a note of the date of death. Please note that it is no longer acceptable to photocopy death certificates. They are crown copyright. Professional practitioners have entered into a protocol with the banks, etc., whereby they send a death notification form containing the details copied from the death certificate. Lay executors administering estates in person will need to purchase extra copies of the death certificate.

The figures given by banks will include interest accrued but not credited at the date of death. This is important for tax purposes.

Liabilities will also need to be ascertained. Credit card bills and the like are deductible for calculating the amount of the estate subject to inheritance tax. The funeral bill is a permitted deduction, as are reasonable expenses for 'mourning' (clothes for the funeral).

Once all the figures have been ascertained, the application for probate may proceed. Usually it will be necessary to fill in a form called an IHT 200 for the Inland Revenue. There is a procedure called the 'excepted estates' procedure whereby estates below a certain level do not have to submit this form. The limit below which this procedure applies is adjusted periodically. At the time of writing, it is set at a level equal to the inheritance tax threshold.

It is essential that the values set out in the IHT 200 are correct. There are stiff penalties for anyone who makes a statement known to be false or recklessly puts down a figure without making 'fullest enquiry' as to its correctness. There are, of course, some assets where the value is very difficult to assess. I once dealt with a very big estate where the deceased had a fondness for modern art. One piece of sculpture, consisting of large pieces of granite, had had to be delivered by crane. He had paid a lot of money for it but nobody wanted to buy it from his estate. Assessing the value for tax purposes proved extremely difficult. Shares in private companies can be very difficult to value, especially where the deceased was a 'key man'. In such circumstances an estimate may be submitted together with details of enquiries made in an effort to obtain a value.

Where an estate is liable for inheritance tax, the Revenue expects the money to be paid upfront. There are two types of assets for tax purposes: 'instalment option' assets and 'non instalment option' assets. Land is an instalment option asset, for example, but cash in the bank is not.

The tax on the non-instalment option assets must be paid to the Cashier's Office of the Capital Taxes Office before the Probate Registry will issue the grant. The Cashier will stamp a receipt onto the form submitted with the IHT 200 and return it for submission with the oath for executors.

The executors' oath is a document reciting the date of the death, the full name and address of the deceased, his age and the reason why the executors claim to be entitled to a Grant of Probate. Where all executors are proving, it will simply say, 'We are the executors named in the will,' but circumstances may arise where further explanation is required. This is usually where the executors making the application are applying under a substitution clause in the will. For example, it is fairly common for a man to appoint his wife executrix in the first instance with a substitute appointment of his children if his wife has died before him. In that instance the oath will recite the fact that the first named executor died during the lifetime of the deceased.

The oath will also state the gross and net values of the estate and contain promises by the executors to give an account of the administration to the court if so required.

It has to be sworn in front of a solicitor other than the one who prepared the papers. The oath contains a statement to the effect that the executors will give an account of the administration to the court and deliver up the grant to the court if so required. It is probably fair to say that most executors who attend before a solicitor to swear the oath do not fully appreciate the seriousness of it. When they promise to give an account of the administration to the court they may not fully appreciate that a disgruntled beneficiary can obtain an order requiring them to do just that. Such orders may be rare but the time and expense involved can be considerable.

If there is no will, the paperwork for a Grant of Letters of Administration is in the same format but recites the applicant's relationship to the deceased and the reason why he is entitled to the grant rather than referring to a will.

Once the oath and IHT receipt have been submitted to the Probate Registry the grant will issue within a couple of weeks. The exact time varies according to which District Registry is used and what the workload there is like.

It is, of course, possible for the executor or proposed administrator to make a personal application for the grant. This involves attending the local Probate Registry in person. The forms are available from the Registry or can be downloaded from the internet in most cases. The forms for inheritance tax have to be completed in the same way. The Capital Taxes Office expects as much attention to precise valuations, etc., to be paid by applicants acting in person as those acting through a solicitor. Personal application is best suited to small, uncomplicated estates although there is nothing to stop the executor of a large estate applying in person.

Once probate has been granted, the will becomes a public document. Anybody can obtain a copy. This is why caution is advisable when writing it in the first place. Your words will live on after your death and may be the source of amusement or ridicule to later generations.

Local newspapers often publish details of wills. These may simply appear under the heading 'Recent Wills' in the public notices column but those considered notable by the editors may be given more prominent treatment. A gift of a large sum to charity is likely to get you a large article and even more so if you have left the money to an animal charity or your own animals. Wills of local dignitaries may likewise receive fuller coverage.

If your relatives do not want your will to be published in the paper, they should write to the editor when the application for probate is submitted. They may only request that the details be omitted; the final decision rests with the editor. Proving the will in a District Registry other than the local one is unlikely to make a lot of difference as to whether the paper picks up the details.

The executor's year

Much annoyance to beneficiaries and probate solicitors alike might be avoided if only this concept were taught at primary school. In essence it means that executors have a year from the date of death during which they are not obliged to pay out to anyone other than the taxman and the undertaker. This gives them time to ascertain assets and liabilities, deal with any problems and draw up estate accounts before distributing the funds to beneficiaries. Liabilities such as utility bills and debts will generally be paid before the end of the year, usually when the estate has been quantified and the statutory notices under s.27 Trustee Act 1925 have expired.

This period is not set in stone. A modest estate might be wound up before the end of the executor's year but a large estate may well continue for a second or third year before the administration is finalised. A house may need to be sold. Foreign assets, ambiguities in the will, missing beneficiaries may all cause problems. Where there are assets such as private company shares that require correspondence with a specialist section of the Inland Revenue, a considerable time may elapse before matters are settled.

Beneficiaries frequently complain of delay because they fail to appreciate the finer points of estate administration. They just want to spend their legacy and become annoyed at what they see as unwarranted delay in sending out the cheques. In fact the executors would not be doing their duty correctly if they paid out before checking that all possible liabilities had been ascertained and dealt with. The last thing any executor wishes to do is to write and ask for some money back because an unexpected liability has arisen.

Wise executors pay heed to two time-limits in particular. The first relates to creditors. A notice to creditors should be placed in the *London Gazette* and a newspaper circulating in the area in which the deceased resided. Such a notice gives creditors two months from the date of publication to notify the executors of their claim against the estate. Executors placing such notices are protected from personal liability for the debts should a valid claim arise later. In this connection it should be noted that the Recovery From Estates section of the Department of Work and Pensions is notoriously slow in writing to claim back overpaid state benefits so that it is advisable to write to them immediately the death occurs.

The other time-limit is the six-month time-limit under the Inheritance (Provision for Family and Dependants) Act 1975. Those six months run from the date of the Grant of Probate not the death. If it takes two months from the death to obtain probate, then the time-limit will not expire until eight months or so after the death. It is a very unwise executor who pays out before the time-limit expires. It may be thought unlikely that a claim will arise but it is never possible to say with certainty. Beneficiaries must understand that it is better to wait out the six months than to be asked to give back money paid out too early because a claim has arisen.

Where an estate has paid inheritance tax, a prudent executor will obtain a tax clearance certificate from the Capital Taxes Office before distributing the estate.

It may happen that a beneficiary will offer to indemnify the executors against any claims that arise if only they will pay out earlier. Great caution should be exercised. There is a well-known case of a solicitor executor who accepted an indemnity from a beneficiary in respect of instalments of inheritance tax. When the beneficiary later went bankrupt and couldn't pay the tax, the Inland Revenue looked to the solicitor to pay it. As the primary responsibility for tax payments rests with the executors he had to pay. The more the beneficiary pleads that he has desperate need of the funds, the more caution should be exercised by the executors. Where the beneficiary concerned is a major charity, the possibility of a default may be far less of a consideration for the executors. In that instance, an indemnity may be offered and considered acceptable. A lot depends on the overall position of the estate and, in particular, whether the charity is sole beneficiary. The final decision must always rest with the executors.

Deeds of variation
Circumstances may change between the time the testator makes his will and the time he dies. His estate may increase or decrease. Family quarrels which led to the exclusion of a child may long since have healed. Leaving a lot of money to a beneficiary who has considerable money of his own may simply create a tax problem in his own estate. Currently it is possible to enter into a deed of variation, also known as a deed of family arrangement, to vary the terms of the will. By statutory concession the revised will is deemed to have been made by the testator himself. It is thus possible to rewrite the terms of the will so as to direct money to beneficiaries who are exempt from tax or to set up a trust of the nil rate band. The variation is effective for inheritance tax purposes and, in many cases, capital gains tax purposes as well, depending on the terms of the variation. For all other purposes, the money which is redirected is a gift from the beneficiary who loses it to the new beneficiary who receives it. For instance, a widow

could not arrange a deed of variation so as to divest herself of assets in order to qualify for local authority funding for care fees.

A beneficiary may also disclaim a legacy by signing a deed of disclaimer. In that event it is the specific gift which is disclaimed. A beneficiary may not disclaim in favour of another.

Both a disclaimer and a deed of variation are post-death arrangements but may be drawn up prior to probate if required.

Professional advice will always be necessary before a deed of variation is entered into, not least because such deeds are most usually made when inheritance tax is a major consideration. The deed must also be correctly worded in order to comply with the relevant legislation. In particular, it must show that the parties involved intend the appropriate sections of the Inheritance Tax Act 1984 and Taxation of Chargeable Gains Act to apply.

SIMPLE FORM OF ASSETS LOG

In the hope that it will prove of some assistance to my executors, I have drawn up this list of my investments, my outstanding bills and the whereabouts of my important documents.

My full name ....
Date and place of birth ....
National insurance number ....
Tax office and reference ....
Current bank account details ....
....
....

Savings account details
Account no.   Bank/Building Society   Address
....
....
....

Shareholdings and investments
I hold shares in the following companies ....
....
....
My share certificates are held in safe custody at ....
....
Other investments ....
....
My house deeds are held at ....
Liabilities
Credit card numbers and addresses ....
....
Utilities ....
Mortgage account ....
Other liabilities ....

CHECKLIST FOR SEEING A SOLICITOR

1. Full name and address plus details of any other name by which you have been known or are currently known.
2. Details of the value of your estate. Values need not be absolutely precise but should be as up to date as possible. The latest statement from the asset-holder will suffice for this purpose.
3. Details of whether assets are held in your sole name, your spouse's sole name or jointly.
4. Names and addresses of the people you wish to appoint as executors.
5. Names and addresses of guardians if you have minor children.
6. Names of people to whom you wish to leave pecuniary or specific legacies, together with details of amounts.
7. The name of the residuary beneficiary and details of alternative beneficiaries should he or she predecease you.
8. Details of any funeral requirements you wish to put in.
9. Any other special provisions you wish to include.

Once you have completed the will with the solicitor, it is helpful to give him a list of assets and liabilities to keep with it. The Law Society publishes a special form for this purpose which is used by some solicitors but is not essential. A straightforward list on a piece of paper, as per the example Simple Form of Assets Log on page 129, will suffice.

SAMPLE WILLS

How to use the sample wills on the following pages

The following pages contain examples of wills drafted to meet a variety of common situations. They cover such matters as appointments of testators and guardians, legacies to executors, grandchildren or friends and various gifts of residue. In addition, each will gives an indication of different funeral wishes so as to illustrate how to express what you want.

Each will is written as if drawn up by a man. If you are a woman leaving a gift to your husband, just substitute the word 'husband' for the word 'wife' and the word 'executor' for the word 'executrix' where appropriate in the sample text. Remember also to change 'his' to 'her' in the attestation clause.

At each point where a person is named as executor or beneficiary you should insert his or her full name and address.

It would be impossible to give an example of each and every type of will a testator may wish to make. It is, therefore, possible that you will need to amend some of the clauses or swap clauses between wills.

You must have:

1. The heading i.e. 'This is the last will and testament [etc.]'.
2. The clause revoking former wills.
3. The appointment of executors.

4. A clause giving the residue of your estate to a beneficiary or group of beneficiaries.
5. The 'in witness' statement which includes the date.
6. The attestation clause, i.e. 'signed by the said [etc]'.

In between the appointment of executors and the residue clause, you may wish to add a gift of money or a specific object, such as your car, to a named beneficiary. You may also wish to appoint a guardian or guardians for your children. After the residue clause and before the 'in witness' statement, you may wish to insert your funeral wishes. Remember to authorise your executors to pay for a memorial if you want one.

Remember that these wills are intended for people with very straightforward affairs. Do not attempt to set up any complicated trust arrangements. The only trust set out in the sample wills is a very simple trust to provide for your pet's welfare after your death. Do not try and change this to apply to your spouse or children.

If you are in any doubt as to how to proceed, or whether the examples given are appropriate in your situation, please seek professional advice, do not attempt to make your own will.

Will giving entire estate to spouse with gift over to son

THIS IS THE LAST WILL AND TESTAMENT of me
.... of ....

1.   I revoke all previous wills made by me

2.   Subject to the payment of my debts funeral expenses and admin-
      istration expenses I give all my estate both real and personal to my
      wife .... and appoint her sole executrix of this my will

3.   If my wife dies before me or the gift to her shall fail for any other
      reason then subject to payment of my debts funeral expenses and
      administration expenses I give all my estate both real and per-
      sonal to my son .... of .... and appoint him
      sole executor of this my will

4.   I wish to be cremated and have my ashes scattered

IN WITNESS whereof I have signed this my will this .... day of
[month year]

Signed by the said .... as his last will in the presence of us both being present at the same time who at his request and in his presence and in the presence of each other have hereunto signed our names as witnesses	[Signature of testator] [Signature of first witness] [Name, address and occupation of first witness] [Signature of second witness] [Name, address and occupation of second witness]

Will appointing friends as executors with everything to spouse and gift over to children

THIS IS THE LAST WILL AND TESTAMENT of me
.... of ....

1.   I revoke all previous wills made by me
2.   I appoint my friends .... of ....
and .... of .... to be the executors and trustees of this my will ('my trustees')
3.   If my wife .... survives me by 28 days then subject to payment of my debts funeral and testamentary expenses I give everything I own to her absolutely provided that if she shall fail to survive me by 28 days or the gift to her shall fail for any other reason the following clauses shall then apply
4.   I give everything I own at my death to my trustees upon the following trusts
    (a)   to pay my debts funeral and testamentary expenses and any tax due as a result of my death
    (b)   to divide my residuary estate between such of my children as are living at my death and if more than one in equal shares
    (c)   in the event of any of my children dying before me leaving a child or children alive at my death then such child or children shall take in equal shares the share that his her or their parent would have taken if he or she had survived me
5.   I wish to be buried after a service in my local church and request that the hymn 'How great thou art' be sung

IN WITNESS whereof I have signed this my will this .... day of [month year]

Signed by the said .... as   [Signature of testator]
his last will in the presence of us   [Signature of first witness]
both being present at the same   [Name, address and occupation of
time who at his request and in   first witness]
his presence and in the presence   [Signature of second witness]
of each other have hereunto   [Name, address and occupation of
signed our names as witnesses   second witness]

Will with legacies to grandchildren, residue to wife and gift over to charity on her death

THIS IS THE LAST WILL AND TESTAMENT of me
.... of ....

1. I hereby revoke all my former wills
2. I appoint my sons .... of .... and .... of .... to be the executors and trustees of this my will ('my trustees')
3. I give the sum of five hundred pounds free of tax to each of my grandchildren living at my death and direct that if they are under 18 at the time of my death my trustees shall accept a receipt from their parents without any responsibility for seeing that the money is applied for their benefit
4. Subject to the payment of my debts funeral and testamentary expenses and the legacies in clause 3 above I give all my residuary estate to my wife .... if she is living at my death provided always that if she shall die before me or the gift to her shall fail for any other reason the following clauses shall take effect
5. Subject as set out in the previous clause I give all my residuary estate to XYZ Cat Sanctuary of .... registered charity no .... and direct that the receipt of the treasurer or other apparently duly authorised officer thereof shall be a good discharge to my trustees
6. I wish to be buried after a Roman Catholic service and I authorise my executors to pay for a headstone for my grave

IN WITNESS whereof I have signed this my will this .... day of [month year]

Signed by the said .... as his last will in the presence of us both being present at the same time who at his request and in his presence and in the presence of each other have hereunto signed our names as witnesses	[Signature of testator] [Signature of first witness] [Name, address and occupation of first witness] [Signature of second witness] [Name, address and occupation of second witness]

Will in contemplation of marriage, estate to spouse with gift over to children of marriage, if any, and alternative gift of residue

I .... make this will in contemplation of my forthcoming marriage with .... and intend that it shall not be revoked by such marriage

1.   I hereby revoke all previous wills I have made
2.   Subject to payment of all my debts funeral and testamentary expenses I give all my estate to the said .... absolutely and appoint her sole executrix thereof and I intend that this gift shall take effect whether or not our marriage has been solemnised at the time of my death
3.   If the said .... should predecease me or the gift to her shall fail for any other reason then the following clauses shall apply
4.   I appoint my brother .... of .... and my sister .... of .... to be the executors and trustees of this my will ('my trustees')
5.   I give all my estate both real and personal whatsoever and wheresoever to my trustees upon trust
     (a)   to pay my debts funeral and testamentary expenses
     (b)   to hold my residuary estate for any children of my marriage to .... who shall be living at my death and attain the age of 18 and if more than one in equal shares
     (c)   in the event of there being no surviving children of our marriage or there being children who fail to live to 18 my trustees shall pay my residuary estate to such of my brothers and sisters as are living at my death and if more than one in equal shares
6.   I desire to be buried and authorise the cost of a memorial stone to be charged to my estate

IN WITNESS whereof I have signed this my will this .... day of [month year]

Signed by the said .... as his last will in the presence of us both being present at the same time who at his request and in his presence and in the presence of each other have hereunto signed our names as witnesses	[Signature of testator] [Signature of first witness] [Name, address and occupation of first witness] [Signature of second witness] [Name, address and occupation of second witness]

Will for cohabitants

THIS IS THE LAST WILL AND TESTAMENT of me
.... of ....

1.   I revoke all my former wills
2.   I appoint .... of .... and .... of
       .... to be my executors and trustees ('my trustees')
3.   Subject to payment of my debts funeral and testamentary
       expenses and any tax arising by reason of my death I give all my
       estate to .... of .... if she survives me by 28 days
4.   If the said .... shall not survive me by 28 days or the gift to
       her shall fail for any reason I give my estate both real and
       personal whatsoever and wheresoever to my trustees to collect in
       and hold upon trust
       (a)   to pay my debts funeral and testamentary expenses and any
               tax due as a result of my death
       (b)   to hold my residuary estate for any children born of my
               relationship with the said .... who survive me and reach
               18 and if more than one in equal shares
       (c)   in the event of there being no children of our relationship or
               there being children who die before the age of 18 my
               trustees shall pay my residuary estate to my friend
               .... of ....
5.   It is my wish that no religious service be held after my death and
       that I be cremated after a simple funeral at which the song 'XYZ'
       by ABC Band is played

IN WITNESS whereof I have signed this my will this .... day of
[month year]

Signed by the said .... as his   [Signature of testator]
last will in the presence of us   [Signature of first witness]
both being present at the same   [Name, address and occupation of
time who at his request and in   first witness]
his presence and in the presence   [Signature of second witness]
of each other have hereunto   [Name, address and occupation of
signed our names as witnesses   second witness]

*Note this will envisages that children will be born in the future. If there are
already children of the relationship, a guardian should be appointed. It is
not usual to name a guardian unless there are already children alive. The
birth of a child, especially the first, is an occasion for updating your will.*

Will with absolute gift to spouse, appointment of testamentary guardian, gift to children and provision for loan to guardian

THIS IS THE LAST WILL AND TESTAMENT of me
.... of ....

1. I hereby revoke all my previous wills
2. After payment of my debts funeral and testamentary expenses I give all my estate to my wife .... and appoint her sole executrix of this my will provided that if she shall predecease me or the gift to her shall fail for any other reason the following clauses shall come into effect
3. I appoint .... of .... and .... of .... to be my executors and trustees ('my trustees')
4. I appoint .... to be the testamentary guardian of any of my children who are minors
5. After paying my debts funeral and testamentary expenses and any taxes due on my death my trustees shall hold my estate upon trust for such of my children living at my death as shall attain the age of 18 and if more than one in equal shares
6. I request that if my trustees consider my children's guardian needs financial assistance to purchase an alternative house to accommodate them or to extend her existing house for that purpose they make funds available to her by way of a loan from my estate on such terms as to repayment and interest as they in their discretion think fit
7. I wish to be cremated after a service at Anytown Parish Church and I authorise my executors to pay for a reception afterwards at a convenient hotel or restaurant

IN WITNESS whereof I have signed this my will this .... day of [month year]

Signed by the said .... as his last will in the presence of us both being present at the same time who at his request and in his presence and in the presence of each other have hereunto signed our names as witnesses	[Signature of testator] [Signature of first witness] [Name, address and occupation of first witness] [Signature of second witness] [Name, address and occupation of second witness]

Will with pecuniary and specific legacies, absolute gift of residue

THIS IS THE LAST WILL AND TESTAMENT of me
.... of ....

1. I revoke all my previous wills
2. I appoint .... of .... and .... of .... to be the executors and trustees of this my will ('my trustees')
3. I give any motor car which I may own at my death to my friend .... of .... free of tax and costs of delivery
4. I give the following monetary gifts free of tax
    (a) £1000 to each of my executors who prove my will
    (b) £2000 to my friend .... of ....
    (c) £5000 to XYZ Cancer Charity of .... registered charity number .... and direct that the receipt of the treasurer or other apparently duly authorised officer thereof shall be a good receipt for my trustees
5. After payment of my debts funeral and testamentary expenses and the legacies in Clause 4 my trustees shall pay my residuary estate to my sister .... of .... absolutely
6. If my sister dies before me my trustees shall pay my residuary estate to my nephew ....of ....
7. If XYZ Cancer Charity shall have ceased to exist at the time of my death I wish my trustees to pay the sum of £5000 to the charity which in their opinion most nearly fulfils the same objects
8. I desire to be buried in the family grave no 1234 at Anytown Churchyard and for my estate to pay for adding my name to the headstone

IN WITNESS whereof I have signed this my will this .... day of [month year]

Signed by the said .... as his last will in the presence of us both being present at the same time who at his request and in his presence and in the presence of each other have hereunto signed our names as witnesses	[Signature of testator] [Signature of first witness] [Name, address and occupation of first witness] [Signature of second witness] [Name, address and occupation of second witness]

Will leaving residue to children with provision for pets for life

THIS IS THE LAST WILL AND TESTAMENT of me
.... of ....

1. I hereby revoke all former wills made by me

2. I appoint .... of .... and .... of .... to be
    the executors and trustees of this my will ('my trustees')

3. I give the sum of £500 free of tax to each of the said .... and
    .... who prove my will

4. I entrust the care of any cats and dogs living with me at my death
    to my brother .... of .... with the request that he takes
    care of them for the rest of their natural lives

5. If my said brother .... is unwilling or unable to take care of
    my animals as requested then I direct my trustees to find an
    alternative carer for them including approaching the local animal
    shelter if necessary and it is my wish that they be kept together for
    the rest of their natural lives

6. I give all my property both real and personal whatsoever and
    wheresoever situate which I own at my death or over which I have
    a power of disposal to my trustees upon trust to collect in the
    same and hold it upon trust

    (a) to pay my debts funeral and testamentary expenses and all
         taxes arising by reason of my death

    (b) to pay the legacies set out in clause 3 above

    (c) to pay ninety per cent of my residuary estate to such of my
         children .... of .... and .... of .... as are
         living at my death and if more than one in equal shares

    (d) (i)   to invest the remaining ten per cent of my residuary
              estate ('the trust fund') in any of the investments
              permitted by law for trustee investment for a period of
              21 years from my death or until the death of the last
              surviving cat or dog residing with me at my death
              whichever is the shorter period

(ii)   to pay to my said brother .... or other
person or organisation having the care of my cats
and dogs so much of the income from the trust fund
as is necessary to pay for their food veterinary care
and other expenses any surplus income to be
accumulated

(iii)   my trustees shall have the power to resort to capital if
the income in any year is inadequate to pay all the said
expenses and for the avoidance of doubt I declare that
the term other expenses shall include payment of up
to three weeks' boarding kennel fees in any calendar
year to enable the carer to go on holiday

(iv)   from and after the death of the last surviving cat or
dog my trustees shall hold the trust fund both capital
and income for such of my children as are then living
and if more than one in equal shares

7.   I desire to be buried with my late wife in grave number 1234 at
Main Road Cemetery Anytown

IN WITNESS whereof I have signed this my will this .... day of
[month year]

Signed by the said .... as his   [Signature of testator]
last will in the presence of us   [Signature of first witness]
both being present at the same   [Name, address and occupation of
time who at his request and in   first witness]
his presence and in the presence   [Signature of second witness]
of each other have hereunto   [Name, address and occupation of
signed our names as witnesses   second witness]

Will giving jewellery to daughters equally, contingent legacies to grandchildren and residue to children

THIS IS THE LAST WILL AND TESTAMENT of me
.... of ....

1.   I hereby revoke all former wills made by me and declare this to be my last will

2.   I appoint my friend .... of .... and my cousin .... to be the executors and trustees of this my will ('my trustees')

3.   I give my jewellery to my trustees to divide between my daughters as they shall in their absolute discretion think fit provided that so far as possible my daughters shall each receive jewellery to the same value and I direct that in the event of any dispute the decision of my trustees shall be final and binding on all parties

4.   I give the sum of £500 to each of my grandchildren who shall survive me and attain the age of 18 years and I direct that such legacies shall carry the intermediate income

5.   Subject to payment of my debts funeral and testamentary expenses and all taxes arising from my death and payment of the legacies mentioned in clauses 3 and 4 hereof I give all my estate both real and personal whatsoever and wheresoever to such of my children .... and .... as are living at my death and if more than one in equal shares

6.   I desire to be cremated and have my ashes scattered over my garden

IN WITNESS whereof I have signed this my will this .... day of [month year]

Signed by the said .... as his last will in the presence of us both being present at the same time who at his request and in his presence and in the presence of each other have hereunto signed our names as witnesses	[Signature of testator] [Signature of first witness] [Name, address and occupation of first witness] [Signature of second witness] [Name, address and occupation of second witness]

Note: In this example the grandchildren have not been named so as to allow for the possibility of further births before the testator's death. This may well be a consideration if the testator's children are still young. If it is fairly certain that no further grandchildren will be born, it is better to name them by inserting their details after the word 'grandchildren' in clause 4.

Will with various specific and pecuniary legacies and residue to charity, one lay executor and one professional

THIS IS THE LAST WILL AND TESTAMENT of me
.... of ....

1.   I hereby revoke all former wills made by me
2.   I appoint my friend .... and the partners at the date of my death in the firm of DEF solicitors of .... or the firm which at the date of my death has succeeded to and carries on its practice to be my executors and trustees ('my trustees') and I direct that only one such partner shall initially prove my will and act in the trusts hereof
3.   I give the following specific legacies free of tax and costs of delivery
     (a)   my diamond and sapphire necklace to my niece .... of ....
     (b)   my emerald brooch to my sister .... of ....
     (c)   my string of pearls to my niece .... of ....
     (d)   my Wedgwood vase to my friend .... of ....
4.   I give the following pecuniary legacies free of tax
     (a)   £500 to my said niece ....of ....
     (b)   £1000 to my nephew .... of ....
5.   I give all the remainder of my estate both real and personal wheresoever and whatsoever to my trustees to collect in and to hold upon trust
     (a)   to pay my debts funeral and testamentary expenses and the legacies set out in clause 4 hereof
     (b)   to pay my residuary estate to the ABC charity of .... registered charity no .... and I direct that the receipt of the treasurer or other duly authorised officer thereof shall be a good discharge to my trustees
6.   I direct that in the event of the said ABC having ceased to exist at the time of my death or having changed its name or amalgamated with some other organisation my trustees shall pay my residuary estate to such organisation as they in their absolute discretion consider most nearly represents the aims of the said ABC charity which I intended to benefit
7.   I wish my burial to be a grand affair with a horsedrawn hearse and a piper to play a lament as my coffin is lowered

IN WITNESS etc.

APPENDIX

Guide to the rights on intestacy for deaths on or after 1st December 1993

The classes are listed in the order of priority. To find out who inherits, work your way down through each class, stopping at the first class which applies. For example, if the deceased was not survived by both spouse and children, but was survived by children only, then that class applies and the children take everything in equal shares regardless of whether there are more distant relatives, such as parents, siblings or grandparents.

Where there is a surviving spouse, then regardless of the size of the estate no person remoter than the issue of brothers and sisters of the whole blood of the intestate are entitled to anything.

The sum received by the surviving spouse is known as 'the statutory legacy'. The amount of the statutory legacy is periodically increased. The increases have not kept pace with house prices amongst other things and another increase in the legacy is overdue. The value of the house will be part of the legacy if it was held in the sole name of the deceased. Assets passing by survivorship do not count towards the statutory legacy. An asset is said to pass by survivorship if it is held in joint names and on a joint tenancy basis so that it is understood by both parties to be the property of the surviving co-owner on the death of the first.

Surviving relatives
SPOUSE AND CHILDREN
Spouse receives:

1.   Personal chattels.
2.   £125,000 free of inheritance tax plus interest at 6 per cent until payment or appropriation.
3.   A life interest in half the remainder with a gift over to children; the other half is given to the children absolutely.

CHILDREN ONLY
Children take in equal shares. Deceased children are replaced by their children.

SPOUSE AND PARENTS
Spouse receives:

1.   The personal chattels.
2.   £200,000 free of inheritance tax plus interest at 6 per cent as above.
3.   Half the remainder absolutely.

The parents take the other half in equal shares.

PARENTS ONLY
The parents take everything in equal shares.

SPOUSE AND SIBLINGS OF THE WHOLE BLOOD
The spouse receives:

1.   The personal chattels.
2.   £200,000 free of inheritance tax plus interest as before.
3.   Half the remainder absolutely.

The siblings take the other half in equal shares. Deceased siblings are replaced by their issue.

SIBLINGS OF THE WHOLE BLOOD ONLY
Siblings take everything in equal shares with deceased siblings being replaced by their issue.

SPOUSE AND SIBLINGS OF THE HALF-BLOOD
Spouse takes everything.

SIBLINGS OF THE HALF-BLOOD
The siblings of the half-blood take everything between them with deceased siblings being replaced by their issue.

SPOUSE AND GRANDPARENTS
Spouse takes everything.

GRANDPARENTS ONLY
Grandparents take everything in equal shares.

SPOUSE AND UNCLES AND AUNTS OF THE WHOLE BLOOD
All to the spouse.

UNCLES AND AUNTS OF THE WHOLE BLOOD ONLY
The uncles and aunts take everything equally with their issue stepping into their place if they have predeceased.

SPOUSE AND UNCLES AND AUNTS OF THE HALF-BLOOD
Spouse takes everything.

UNCLES AND AUNTS OF THE HALF-BLOOD ONLY
The uncles and aunts of the half-blood share everything between them, with any who predeceased the intestate being replaced by their issue.

NO RELATIVES IN ANY OF THE ABOVE CLASSES BUT SPOUSE SURVIVES
The spouse receives everything.

No Spouse and no relatives in any of the above
classes
Everything to the Crown, the Duchy of Lancaster or the
Duke of Cornwall depending on residence.

Charities and will making

There is a scheme operated by Cancer Research, the
charity which was formed by the joining together of
the Imperial Cancer Research Fund and Cancer Research
UK. The charity has agreed rates for a standard will with
participating solicitors. The way the scheme works is that
the charity pays for your will in the hope that you will
leave it a legacy. Due to something called the benefit/
bounty rule there can be no compulsion for you to leave a
legacy even though the charity is expending its funds on
paying your solicitor to write your will for you. A list of
participating solicitors may be obtained from the charity.

The other scheme is called Will Aid and operates for a
limited period every other year. This involves solicitors
volunteering to join the scheme; their names being made
available to the public by the organisers. The solicitor will
make your will for nothing but you must agree to donate
the cost of it to the Will Aid campaign. The money
donated is shared between Actionaid, the British Red
Cross, Christian Aid, Help The Aged, the NSPCC, Save
The Children UK, SCIAF (Scotland) and Trocaire
(Northern Ireland). The suggested donation of £65 for a
single will and £95 for husband and wife wills covers a
basic will only. More complex wills may be drawn up but
will involve an additional payment to the solicitor. Each
participating solicitor will only make so many wills under
this scheme each time it operates. Look out for posters and
adverts in your area.

Some other charities have lists of solicitors who have
agreed to give their supporters advice on wills at a special
(usually discounted) rate. Their literature will usually mention this. Other charities, such as The Leprosy Mission,

have details of solicitors sympathetic to their aims which are made available to their supporters.

Inheritance tax rates

For the tax year 2004/2005 the threshold at which inheritance tax starts to bite is £263,000. Any estate over and above that level is taxed at 40 per cent. Liabilities such as credit card bills and funeral costs are deducted from the value of the deceased's estate before calculating the tax liability. In addition to the threshold of £263,000, there is an annual exemption of £3,000 available to everyone during their lifetime. This may be carried forward for one year only. For example, if no gifts are made in the tax year 2004/05 gifts to the value of £6,000 may be made in the tax year 2005/06 without biting into the taxpayer's nil rate band of £263,000.

There are other, more minor, exemptions which apply to lifetime giving. For example, a parent may give £5,000 to a child on marriage. A grandparent may give £2,500 to a grandchild on marriage.

Gifts to registered charities are exempt from inheritance tax, whether made during life or by will.

GLOSSARY

Administrator   Person authorised by the court to administer the estate of someone who dies without making a will.

Administratrix   Female version of administrator.

Affidavit   A statement which is confirmed by oath or affirmation.

Animus testandi   The intention to create a will.

Assets passing by survivorship   Assets in joint names, such as bank accounts, that pass automatically to one owner on the death of the other and not by his will.

Attestation   The clause in a will confirming that the will was signed by the testator in the presence of witnesses.

Beneficiary   Person who benefits under a will or under the intestacy rules.

Codicil   Document changing some aspect of the will but leaving the rest intact.

En ventre sa mere   A child as yet unborn.

Estate   The assets and liabilities left by the deceased.

Executor   Person appointed by will to administer a deceased person's estate.

Extrinsic evidence	Evidence as to the meaning of a will or circumstance of its preparation/execution other than that apparent from the document itself.
Grant of Letters of Administration	Document issued by the court authorising a person to administer the estate of someone who has died intestate.
Grant of Probate	Document issued by the court confirming that a will is the true and last will of a deceased person and confirming the executor's authority to act.
Guardian	Person appointed by will to take the place of a deceased parent.
Half-blood	Relatives of the half-blood have the same parent in common.
Holograph will	Will written in the testator's own handwriting.
Intestacy	Dying without making a will.
Intestate	Person who dies without making a will.
Issue	Children, grandchildren, great-grandchildren, etc.
Legacy	Gift made by will.
Legatee	Person who receives a gift under a will.
Minor	A child under the age of 18 years (21 for wills made before 1970).
Personal chattels	Household effects and items of a similar nature.

Propound a will in court   Hold a will out to be the true and correct last will/seek to prove a will in court.

Prove a will   Apply and be granted a Grant of Probate of a will.

Residue of the estate   What remains of an estate after the payment of all charges, debts and bequests.

Statutory legacy   Amount a spouse receives under the intestacy rules.

Testamentary capacity   The intention and mental capacity to understand the process of making a will as defined by the appropriate legal criteria.

Testator   Person who draws up a will covering the events to happen on his death.

Testatrix   Female version of a testator.

Trustee   Person who administers an ongoing trust set up in a will or during a person's lifetime.

Whole blood   Relatives of the whole blood have both parents in common.

INDEX